Malaga

ANDALUSIA

Andalusia covers some 17% of Spain's surface area (87,268 square metres) and, with a population of 7 million inhabitants, is only slightly smaller than Portugal or Switzerland. The expression "miniature continent" can be applied to Andalusia perhaps more than to any other place given that it is a region of extreme contrasts. Grazalema in the West, for example, is the wettest place in Spain, with an average annual rainfall of over 2000 cubic centimetres, while Cabo de Gata, at the region's eastern end, is the country's driest spot. The year-round snow of the Sierra Nevada mountain range is clearly visible from the market gardens of Andalusia's coastal strip, where tropical fruits such as mangos, avocado pears and custard apples are grown. The vast rocky solitude of the Sierra Morena, isolated to the north by the Meseta, is the very antithesis of the watery paradise of Doñana. Even the ocean is bisected at the Straits of Gibraltar to provide a contrast between the bright, sunny Mediterranean beaches and the Atlantic coastline, along the length of which the wind has erected long dunes of golden sand. These physical differences in turn affect the character of Andalusia's inhabitants, and it is for this reason that people speak of "the two Andalusias", so different one from the other in both physical and human terms. Nevertheless, nobody would for an instant question the unity of vision in the concept of Andalusia, in which there is room only for enriching variety, and not for short-sighted exclusion. This unity is intangible rather than physical and has more to do with the atmosphere of the region, in the way of looking at life and in the spiritual heritage of other cultures, the sediment bequeathed by great civilizations. Lower Andalusia is the western part of the region, the axis of which is the city of Seville, and which is located in the valley of the Guadalquivir River, which meets the Atlantic Ocean at the Gulf of Cadiz. Upper Andalusia, the eastern part of the region, straddles the Bética mountain ranges, and above all the valleys between these ranges, the fertile plains which are home to the area's main towns. Some 17% of the surface area is protected in the form of reserves and natural parks, without taking into account Europe's most important natural park: Doñana. This means that over 20% of the land is completely unspoilt and can be developed in a rational manner. Andalusia's cultural heritage, unsurpassable in terms of richness, is a reflection of the history of the desire for these lands on the part of all the peoples who have invaded Andalusia throughout the ages and who have dotted monuments and ideas across the length and breadth of the region, many of which are landmarks to the development of thought in both the West and the East. A backdrop of such variety and beauty, which has witnessed the birth of such a dazzling wealth of cultural heritage, Andalusia has also had its ups and downs and has suffered centuries of neglect and abandonment at the hands of History. The last quarter of the twentieth century has had a positive effect on the progress of a people whose heritage and cultural wealth this book will attempt to encapsulate.

CORDOBA
JAEN
HUELVA
SEVILLA
GRANADA
ALMERIA
MALAGA
CADIZ
EXTREMADURA
PORTUGAL
Parque Natural de la Sierra de Aracena y Picos de Aroche
Parque Natural de la Sierra Norte de Sevilla
Parque Natural Sierra de Hornachuelos
Medina Azahara
Almonaster la Real
Aracena
Alájar
Gruta de las Maravillas
Cazalla de la Sierra
Constantina
Almodóvar del Río
Río
GUADIANA
Odiel
Tinto
Río
Écija
Carmona
Itálica
Niebla
HUELVA
SEVILLA
Moguer
Palos de la Frontera
Ayamonte
Almonte
Alcalá de Guadaira
Marchena
Puente-Genil
Estepa
Arahal
Osuna
Utrera
El Rocío
Monasterio de la Rábida
Parque Nat. de Doñana
Matalascañas
Parque Nacional de Doñana
Vidal & Vidal
Ediciones Turísticas, S.L.
COSTA DE LA LUZ DE HUELVA
OCEANO
ATLÁNTICO
Parque Nat. de Doñana
Zahara de la Sierra
Acinipo Ronda la Vieja
Parque Natural Sierra de Grazalema
Grazalema
Ubrique
Ronda
Parq. Nat. Sierra de las Nieves
Sanlúcar de Barrameda
Jerez de la Frontera
El Puerto de Sta. Mª
CÁDIZ
Parque Natural Bahía de Cádiz
San Fernando
Marbella
Estepona
Jimena de la Frontera
Parque Natural de los Alcornocales
COSTA DE LA LUZ DE CÁDIZ
Parq. Nat. La Breña y Marismas del Barbate
Ruinas de Baelo Claudia
Algeciras
La Línea de la Concepción
Tarifa
Ante
Mija
COST

MAP OF ANDALUSIA

Above, view of the Nasrid Alcazaba from the Port. This is a good example of the restoration work carried out by Torres Balbás at the beginning of the 20th century and has been a national monument since 1931. Below, the Tres Gracias fountain, a feature which completes the tree-lined walk or Alameda and the subtropical botanical gardens of the gateway Puerta Oscura.

MALAGA

Malaga is known to be a very ancient city, but the exact spot of its original founding is unknown.The town predates the Phoenician, Greek and Roman occupations and has its origins in remote prehistoric times. The cosmopolitan nature of the city over the centuries is immediately apparent. A look at its geographical position on the map is enough to indicate the important role which it played in Mediterranean trade in ancient times and the strategic significance of the town during Muslim times. Malaga became the capital of a Taifa kingdom and was at the centre of the disputes and civil wars of the last Nasrid period, and when the town finally fell to the Christian conquerors in 1487 in the bloodiest battle of that ten-year war, the whole of the

western part of the Granada Kingdom fell with it. Over the centuries Malaga continued to attract seafaring peoples, especially traders from Genoa who founded Spain's very first bank. In the nineteenth century the city was also at the forefront of Spain's industrial revolution which was initiated in Malaga and then moved up to the north of the country. The first half of the twentieth century saw Malaga's economy booming as the capital of Spain's principal industry, tourism, and the cosmopolitan nature of the city will no doubt make it important part of the global village in the course of the present century.

View from Gibralfaro of the Alameda and Port. Below, a nineteenth century photograph by Laurent of the Market and the gate Puerta de las Ataranzas.

The City

This panoramic view of the city with the Cathedral and Gibralfaro in the background (above) sums up the geographical history of the city, skirted by fishermen's districts and by the famous Trinidad and Perchel districts, which have now become showpieces of modern architecture. Historically, the city grew huddled against the slopes of the mountains and around the River Guadalmedina, which was both the city's source of drinking water and an occasional cause of mayhem when its banks flooded. The Gibralfaro Fortress on the lighthouse mountain, despite the delapidated appearance of some of its towers, is actually the newest of the various fortresses which were built on the hill. At the base of the fortress the remains of a Roman theatre can be observed. These ruins were discovered in the twentieth century, but it seems certain that the watchtower guarded over the Port in both Greek and Phoenician eras, given the city's strategic position and trading importance in ancient times. The archaeological exhibits on display in the Archaeological Museum, which is housed in the fortress itself provide a good record of the city's past. The building, which has a distinctly Nasrid air about it, is the very essence of the Mediterranean abode. Here the visitor may observe an extensive collection of archaeological finds such as a monolithic gargoyle *(left)* with a water channel shaped in the form of a snake designed to slow down the water flow. Also on display is the Mihrab Shell from a mosque *(below)*. This shell symbolized water and life, and features in many Islamic mosques. However, it is the Museum's magnificent collection of ceramics which would alone make a visit to the Museum worthwhile.

The Cathedral

Like the city itself, is the product of numerous historical influences. Built on the ruins of the old mosque after the Conquest, it was constructed in the by then declining Gothic style. Unavoidable delays brought its construction forward to the middle of the sixteenth century when Siloé the Renaissance maestro was working on the sanctuary of the Cathedral. The stamp of the maestro can be appreciated in the height of the column bases and in the second row Corinthian columns, which also have very extended bases constructed by his apprentices. This gives the edifice an uplifting aspect which is more often associated with the Gothic style, particularly in the apse (previous page, below), which is diaphanous and spacious because it was never occupied by the choir which was located in the central nave diminishing the perceived size of the interior. Nevertheless, the choir, which is the Cathedral's main architectural attraction, boasts some of the very finest choir stalls, which is to a large extent the work of the sculptor Pedro de Mena, whose genius leaves no doubt as to authorship. The façade (right), which was obviously completed at a later date, is wholly Baroque in concept, even though it retains the triumphal triple arch so typical of the Renaissance which provides a suitably austere framework to the Baroque colour of the marble, the conjunction of columns and finials, the composition of which lightens with the windows and rose windows of the second storey, all of which is highlighted by the dual colour of the stone. Unusually, the naves and ailes of the Cathedral are exactly the same height, as can be observed from maestro Aldehuela's façade.

Malaga Cathedral is an unfinished church, popularly known as the "Manquita". The ups and downs of history meant that the money destined for the second tower was diverted to the Americas to support the United States in the War of Independence in 1776.

Gaucín

The arc of mountains which protects Malaga from the inclemencies of the Continental climate is completed by the Serranía de Ronda to the north-west, which is worthy of its own chapter, a mountainous landscape which proved to be a perfect refuge for bandits. As well as the town of Ronda, the mountain landscape of seemingly impossible sheerness is scattered with remote villages and hamlets which are little visited despite their proximity to the Costa del Sol. As well as Casares, the paradise of the modern architect and designer, the smuggler's route which started in Gibraltar, passed through places such as Gaucín perched on the crest of the mountains (above), Benarrabá, Benadalid and Atajate. Flashes of white amongst the walnut and chestnut trees, the Muslim past of these villages is not limited only to the Moorish architecture (below, Tolox in the Sierra de las Nieves mountains). The sweeping arc of mountains also includes Alpandeire, Faraján, Cartajima, Parauta, and to the west of the river Guadiaro, Cortes de la Frontera, Benaoján and Montejaque which surround the Pileta and Gato Caves whose fascinating cave paintings demonstrate that this area has been highly coveted since the Paleolithic era.

Fuentepiedra

Fuente de Piedra: with a surface area of 1,364 hectares, Andalusia's largest lagoon and resting point for numerous birds, including pink flamingos which use the lagoon as a stopping-off point on their long migratory journeys. It is one of the few important refuges of green Spain. Its water table extends as far as Campillos and the surrounding area (photo above).

Tolox

Pantano del Guadalhorce

Casares

Above is a panoramic view of Caseres, a village of white houses hugging the mountain slopes in the proximity of the Straits of Gibraltar and the essence of popular Andalusian architecture. On the right is Menga Cave in Antequera, an impressive Megalithic monument which dates from the same time as the Egyptian Pyramids and erected with stone slabs weighing up to 180 tons.

Cueva de la Menga

In the north-east of the province, in the valley of the River Guadalhorce we can find the townships of Archidona and Antequera, remote villages which have been inhabited since prehistoric times due to the unbeatable conditions which they offer for human settlement. Situated on high ground, safe from attack, with ample rainfall and dominating fertile surrounding valleys, they were used as granaries in Roman times and were a prize fought over by Moors and Christians as the remains of fortresses in the area bear witness.

THE AXARQUÍA, a word of Arabic origin meaning "east" is the name given to the eastern part of Malaga. Mountainous and blessed with a benign climate, the area is world famous for its sweet wines made from sun-dried raisins. The coast itself is commonly referred to as the "longest street in Europe" with towns and villages such as Vélez Málaga, Nerja with its famous caves *(below right)*, and numerous coves formed where the ravines meet the sea. Less well-known is the mountain area dotted with unpretentious white villages where hundreds of white farmhouses break the green scenery as the traveller rounds every bend in the road. In this area the villages of Frigiliana *(above)*, Cómpeta *(below right)*, Arches and Salares can be found. The latter is noteworthy for its minaret towers and narrow streets of whitewashed houses decorated with flowerpots.

Frigiliana

Cuevas de Nerja

Puerto Banús

La Axarquía

Above, the beach at Fuengirola. Below, the fishing port.

Above, the mole protecting the port

The Costa del Sol

In the 1960's the Costa del Sol, which had up to that time been a peaceful coast of fishing ports, experienced a tourist development boom thanks to its benign climate which would turn it into the Mediterranean's number one tourist destination. In the province of Malaga alone there are over 100 km of beaches and more hotel beds than in the whole of Greece or the old Yugoslavia. The coast boasts modern marinas and the finest range of golf courses in Spain which give an idea of the social and economic potential of a leisure industry which is becoming increasingly related to quality of life. As well as a growing cosmopolitan metropolis, the Costa also covers the villages which are perched in the overlooking mountains where the visitor can discover countless unspoilt spots and drink in their calm, unhurried atmosphere. This is the same relaxed atmosphere which innumerable modern housing complexes have attempted to emulate. Benalmádena and Mijas are two examples of such intelligent development which, despite experiencing the consequences of rapid growth, have managed to retain an air of calmness, Seneca's enviable legacy. Inland from the coast, the white villages perched on mountainsides and hillsides, so near in terms of distance yet so very different, are the vestige of a hard-working rural society of modern crops and unimaginable scenery. A tour around the Alhaurines as far as Coín,

Below, the village of Casares

Above, a whitewashed street in Mijas and, below, the beach

Monda and Ojén is a fascinating experience and the Refugio del Juanar can be found in the vecinity. This authentic natural paradise is located just a few kilometres from Marbella. The small town of Mirivilia, which is amongst the most ancient yet today the most modern in the area, has become in the closing years of the twentieth century the Mediterranean high society capital . The so-called "Golden Mile", with its dazzling appearance, attracts tycoons and leaders of finance from all over the world, as well as aristocrats and stars, whose influence has been a catalyst of economic growth. Such high society personalities have in their turn brought with them a train of opportunists who swarm around this bee-hive of wealth, located a short distance from the tax haven of Gibraltar. A few years ago a motorway was built to ease the traffic on the coast, and it has made the Costa one of the parts of Spain with the best communications. On the shore of the Mediterranean Ocean we can find Torremolinos and Fuengirola, which, apart from being major tourist resorts also conserve their towers and castles and give the impression of having been created since time untold with relaxation in mind. In San Pedro de Alcántara the remains of Andalusia's only Moorish basilica can be found nestling amongst pine and eucalyptus trees. This art form, remnants of which are dotted across the north of mainland Spain, originated here in the ninth century.

Antequera

The Roman name for the region Antikaria gives us an idea of the human presence which has been a constant factor in this region over the centuries and the whiteness of the town of Antequera lords over the area. Antequera has a population of some 45,000 inhabitants and the surrounding region has always been the geographical heart of Andalusia, and as such a crossroads for roads and motorways. The Megalithic cave complex at la MENGA *(page 9)* bears witness to this fact, as do el ROMERAL AND VIERA, all of which are amongst the most important Megalithic remains in Spain. The famous statue of a youth (Efebo) still survives from Roman times. This is a masterpiece sculpted in the first century and can be seen in the Municipal Museum, which is housed in the Nájera Palace. After an early conquest by the Muslims of Granada (1410), the town became the centre of border operations throughout the rest of the fifteenth century, which meant that noble families from Castile settled in the town and enriched the area with the palaces and churches which it boasts today. Santa María la Mayor, in the vecinity of the Alcazaba is an imposing edifice. Also in the same area we encounter the Arco de los Gigantes (Giants' Arch) of gigantic proportions, and, in the main street, the church of San Sebastian, next to the square which is closed off by the Nazarene Arch. The artistic zenith of the town came with the Baroque style and the church, Iglesia del CARMEN is an outstanding example of this art form. THE PORTICHUELO *(right)* is the very essence of the rather unusual Antequera Baroque style which is a dialogue between whitewashed walls and red brickwork.

El Torcal

Just south of Antequera, in the karstic mountains between the town and the sea, Mother Nature has chiselled out a veritable workshop of stone sculptures whose shapes and sizes verge on the fantastical. This area is known as el Torcal, a landscape which has been chastised by erosion since it emerged from the sea, intricate and fanciful, honeycombed with passages and ledges hanging perilously above a sheer drop to the Valley of Abdelacis below.

ARCHIDONA

Another of those townships in which the village's fortress is easily confused with the rock on which it stands, a Medieval rock-castle symbiosis; balconies designed to dominate as far as the horizon. Watching over this pulpit today is the Virgen de Gracia Church, formerly a Caliphate mosque *(tenth century, right)*. This is one of the few surviving mosques from that epoch and it is where the Syrians proclaimed Abderramán I emir. There is a splendid view from this point of the seventeenth century eight-sided Square *(below, right)*.

To the left is el Torcal, a landscape of natural rock sculptures. To the right is el Chorro, a narrow pass leading to the River Guadalhorce.

Paraje de las Pedrizas

Archidona

Mezquita califal, siglo X.

EL CHORRO

Plaza ochavada, Archidona

Reja de forja rondeña

Fachada del Palacio de Salvatierra

Minarete de San Sebastián

RONDA

Escudo de armas en la iglesia de San Francisco

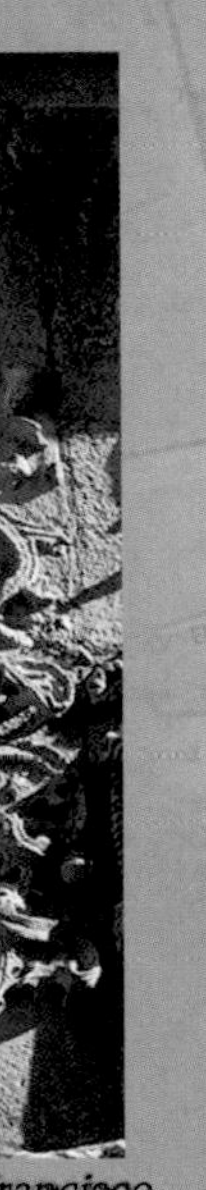

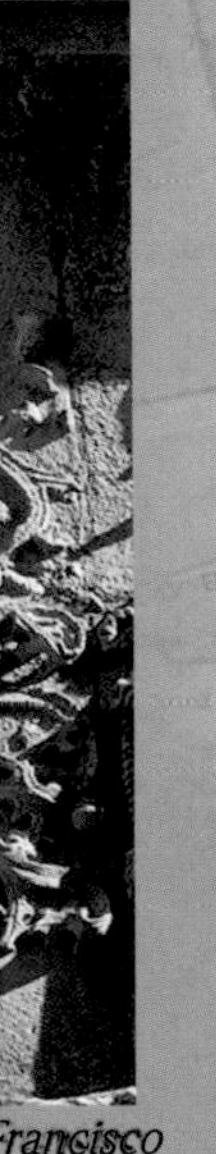

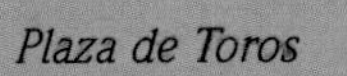

Plaza de Toros

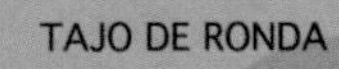

El Tajo

TAJO DE RONDA

NUMENTOS

		RUTA	RUTA
esia Sta. María la Mayor.	10 Casa del Rey Moro.	1 Fuente de los ocho caños.	1 Iglesia del Espíritu Santo.
yuntamiento .	11 Minarete de San Sebastián.	2 Iglesia Padre Jesús .	2 Murallas de Almocabar .
onvento de Sta. Isabel.	12 Palacio Marqués de Salvatierra.	3 Iglesia de la Oscuridad.	3 Puerta de Almocabar.
lacio de Mondragón.	13 Puerta de Felipe V.	4 Posada de las Animas.	4 Puerta de Carlos V.
uralla de la Albacara.	14 Puente viejo.	5 Templete V. de los Dolores.	5 Iglesia Virgen de Gracia.
sa de S. Juan Bosco.	15 Baños árabes.	6 Iglesia de los Descalzos.	6 Convento de Franciscanas.
esia Virgen de la Paz.	16 Puente de San Miguel.	7 Plaza de toros.	7 Convento de San Francisco.
ente Nuevo.	17 Murallas de la Xijára.	8 Iglesia del Socorro.	8 Iglesia Virgen de la Cabeza.
onvento de Sto. mingo.		9 Convento de la Merced.	
		10 Alameda.	
		11 Parador.	

Palacio de Mondragón

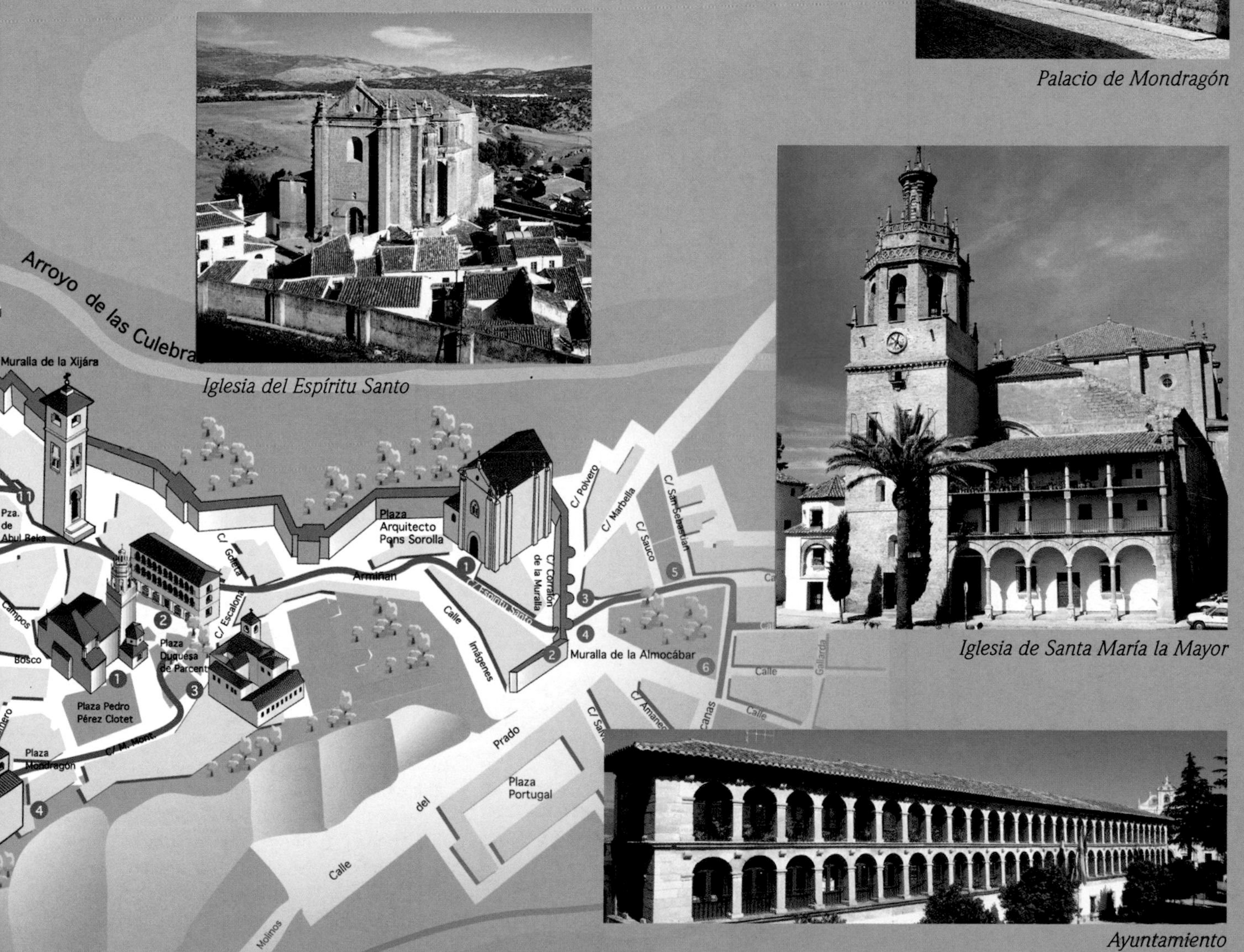

Iglesia del Espíritu Santo

Iglesia de Santa María la Mayor

Ayuntamiento

Vista del Puente Nuevo desde el Parador

RONDA

When approaching Ronda from any direction, the town rears up like a white apparition in the midst of a mountainous ampitheatre hewn out of the rock by some gigantic Vulcan. At a height of 770 metres yet only 50 km from the sea, the town dominates the surrounding meseta which over many centuries was an obligatory route for livestock droves, caravans, smugglers and armies. This explains the importance of the town since prehistoric times: it provided a setting for the Second Punic War between the Romans who bequeathed the area with a magnificent theatre in ARUNDA, Ronda la Vieja (Ronda the Old), at some 13 km distance from the modern town. In the tenth century OMAR BEN HAFSUN, son of Ronda, almost succeeded in defeating the Cordoba Caliphs. The town was the capital of an independent Taifa kingdom during part of the eleventh century and its eventual conquest was only possible with the aid of King Ferdinand the Catholic's Machiavellian subterfuge. Delighted with the conquest of the town in 1485, Ferdinand had the ESPÍRITU SANTO (Holy Spirit) Church constructed next to the gateway Puerta de Almocábar *(above)* which formed part of a formidable protective wall which still partially exists *(top right)*.The town's defences were completed by the impassable gorge and soaring river cliffs of the Guadalevín *(centre)*. In accordance with the customs of the time the mosque, some remains of which can still be seen, was Christianized after the Conquest, to be transformed at a later date into the town's principal church, SANTA MARÍA LA MAYOR, an unusual example of the mixture of Gothic and Renaissance styles. The Muslims left behind them a beautiful minaret as well as the public baths (from the thirteenth to fourteenth centuries), both of which are located close to the river. They also bequeathed the seemingly endless staircase of La Mina in the Casa del Rey Moro (the Moorish King's House) and the Casa del Gigante (the Giant's House) which dates from the same period and is an important example of a Nasrid noble's house. The MONDRAGÓN PALACE, which was the residence of both emirs and Christian kings, later became war booty and was adorned with patios and Renaissance gardens. But it was in the seventeenth and eighteenth centuries that Ronda was transformed into the town which we know today, when, without turning its back on its Moorish past, the town adapted to the manners of modern times: as a major agricultural and trading centre the town witnessed the emergence of churches and convents, at the same time as the new PLAZA DE TOROS (Bull Ring) was constructed completely from stone -in 1784- and the PUENTE NUEVO (New Bridge) was erected. The sturdy and unruly folk of the town, cradle of the smuggler and the bandit of popular folklore, were the first to formalize and regulate that tragic dance of death which is the bull-fight, which in itself presupposes the existance of stockbreeding and aristocratic social classes. The Puente Nuevo (New Bridge) required over 40 years to be erected almost 100 metres above the bottom of the imposing gorge (el Tajo) and was the work of Aldehuela who died at

View of the mountains from the House of D. Bosco

the end of the project (1793). Next to the Arch of Felipe V, which replaced an earlier Arabic gate in the city wall, is the Palace of the Marquis of Salvatierra with its interesting two-section Baroque façade.

Above the typical Ronda-style wrought iron balcony are some unusual and attractive female figures from the West Indies supporting the tympanum which frames the family shield *(above).* A wide corridor leads to an austere inner patio with arches and a Bucolic garden overlooking Ronda. At the bottom of the steep slope the Ronda-style fountain Fuente de los Ocho Caños presides over the square of the Gothic-Herrerian church of Nuestro Padre de Jesús *(right).* This is the starting point of the road leading to the old bridges and the Arabic baths. Every corner offers a different view of the city, such as those of the House of Don Bosco *(above)*, the Hotel Reina Victoria, the Parador, etc

GRANADA

Like so many great cities, its origins lie in ancient times, beyond historical record, a fact which can be explained by a simple glance around the geographic surroundings: Granada lies under lofty mountains, snow-capped throughout the year and guaranteeing vital water supplies, facing a wide, fertile plain providing subsistence even in the most difficult of times, close to the sea, with a mild climate and clear skies during most of the year... This must have been like a dream world for those disembarking to settle in Andalusia, a land that has received so many newcomers. Granada, then, since time immemorial has been a land to be coveted and fought for. In times of peace, settlements were established in the plain, the Vega , and in turbulent times the inhabitants retreated up to the foothills of the Sierra Nevada to create forts or camps that in time became population centres. The ebb and flow of the population followed a logical, almost mathematical pattern: thus, the Romans settled at

Elvira, near the thermal springs of Pinos Puente in the plain, on a site that is rich in prehistoric remains, and where a famous 4th century Church Council was held. There was also a Jewish settlement, Garnat al- Yehudi, and an ancient Moorish Alcazaba, or fortress, on the slopes of the Albayzin, remains of which may still be seen. Granada was of only secondary importance while first the Romans, and then the Moors dominated the Mediterranean; then, the political heartland was in Mérida, Córdoba or Sevilla. Granada was merely an inland paradise to be enjoyed by those far from the centres of influence. However, when the Christians gathered momentum in their campaign to drive the Moorish invaders into the sea, Granada became the centre of the Moors' final stronghold, managing to survive among the mountains of the Penibetic system for over two hundred and fifty years as an (almost) independent kingdom. This was one of those epochs, rare though not unique in history, during which man dedicated his energies, not just to obtaining sustenance, but also to cultivating the spirit, reaching heights of achievement that are still admired today.

Tabernacle of the Carthusian Monastery

Façade of the Royal Hospital

Cloister of the Monastery of St. Jerome

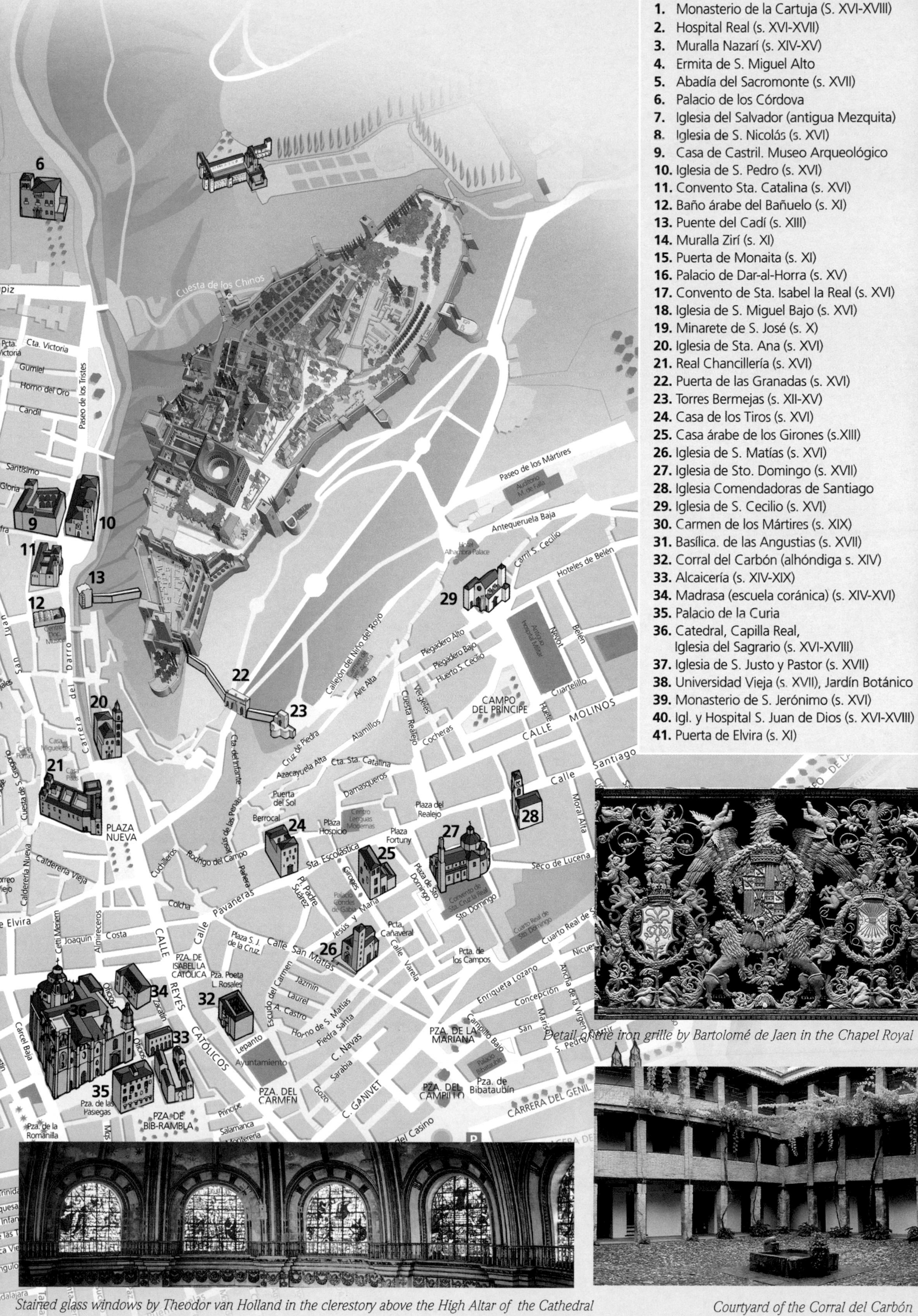

Detail of the iron grille by Bartolomé de Jaen in the Chapel Royal

Stained glass windows by Theodor van Holland in the clerestory above the High Altar of the Cathedral

Courtyard of the Corral del Carbón

Panorama of the Alhambra and Granada from the Albaizin

The Alhambra

Dominating the Red Hill, or Cerro de la Sabika , the fortress known as the Alhambra rises up, proud and eternal, one of the most important architectural achievements of the Middle Ages and the most exquisite example of Islamic art on European soil. The hilltop that provides a pedestal for the Alhambra is an irregular triangle which to the east is bounded by the Cerro del Sol, above which are the Generalife gardens and Silla del Moro. The northern limit of this triangle is formed by the River Darro, while to the west is the Alcazaba fortress and to the south, the "Molten Silver Divide", which today is the central path through the woods of the Alhambra, the Cerro del Mauror and the Torres Bermejas (the Vermilion Towers).

The hill on which the Alhambra is constructed, with an altitude of over two thousand feet above sea level, is a torrential derivation of the Sierra Nevada formed by detritic schists and quartz. The alluvial materials it contains never reached the stage of rock-formation, but have provided a firm, solid base for the Alhambra for many centuries. It is shaped like a ship whose prow, formed by the Alcazaba, points towards the city it will never reach, with a length of 700m. from the Alcazaba to the tower of Cabo de la Carrera and a maximum width of almost 200m. The whole complex has an area of some 13 hectares, and is surrounded by over 2 km. of walls, reinforced by thirty watchtowers, some of which are today in ruins.

To date, apart from the abstract references of some descriptions within the Alhambra itself, no Arab text referring to the Alhambra has been found, unless we accept as such the exclamations to be found in the correspondence of some of the kings of Granada, such as "We write from the Alhambra of Granada, may God preserve her!". There is nothing else.

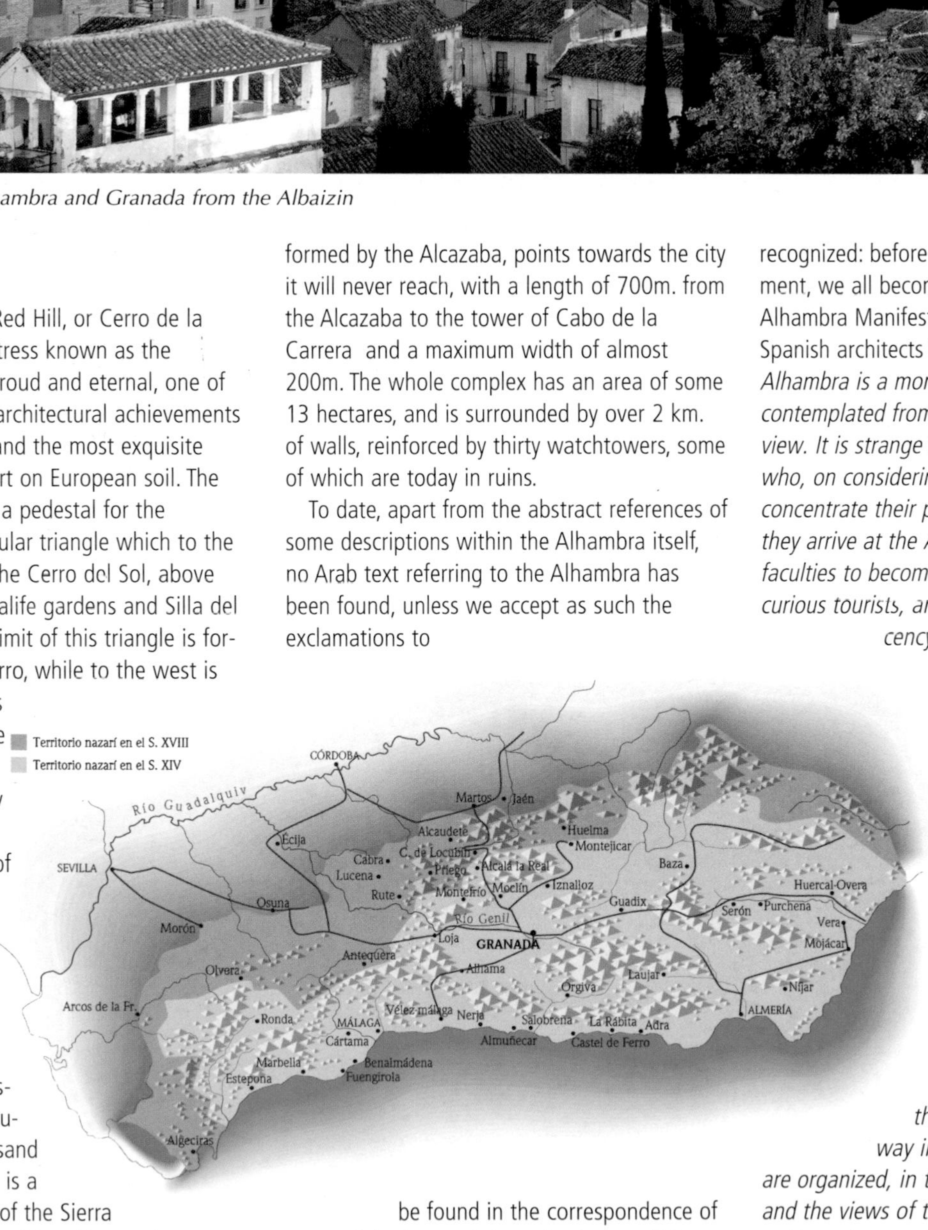

The significance of the Alhambra in architectural terms has not always been sufficiently recognized: before the grandeur of the monument, we all become simple tourists. The Alhambra Manifesto, subscribed by a group of Spanish architects in 1953, states *"The Alhambra is a monument that has never been contemplated from the architectural point of view. It is strange that even architects, those who, on considering the Escorial sharpen and concentrate their professional scrutiny, when they arrive at the Alhambra, relax their critical faculties to become just another group of curious tourists, and even excuse their complacency by distinguishing their professional judgement from their emotions. They say, Yes, I like that, but not as architecture".* Later, on pages 13 and 14 of the same text, one reads, *"The relationship between this 14th century building and contemporary, more advanced, architecture is, in some instances, astonishing. They coincide in their acceptance of the human scale, in the asymmetric but organic way in which the different levels are organized, in the way in which the gardens and the views of the landscape are incorporated into the complex, in the economical, austere use (with no frippery or padding) of materials, and in so many other ways".* Despite its classical origins, the Alhambra, in fact, is in its conception and in the way it is constructed an

Below, aerial view of the Alhambra

architectural complex of the utmost modernity. The Swiss architect Le Corbusier found here a concrete example of his definition of modern architecture as "the intelligent, correct and magnificent combination of volumes brought together under the sun", a theory he described as ideal in his 'Cité Moderne' (1922). In his constructions, he attempted to bring the garden and the landscape within the building and his yardstick was always the human scale.

Francisco Prieto Moreno, who for many years was the architect responsible for the conservation of the monument, said, "In its different sections, the Alhambra combines a variety of architectural values that are still effective and, of course, considered to be works of genius". Another constructional achievement is that the palaces of the Alhambra, of different epochs and constructed on a highly irregular foundation, maintain the perpendicularity of the axes of the patios, thus creating a regular, harmonious whole.

In fact, the Alhambra grew steadily from one century to the next, and with every day that passed its splendour increased: it was not planned from the start as a single unit made up of various elements, but rather was derived from the Alcazaba fortress that dated back to the end of the 9th century. A hundred years later, during the reigns of the great constructors Yusuf I and his son Muhammad V -particularly during the last years of the latter's reign- the Alhambra was already outstanding, white and dazzling like a sunbeam on the gardens of the Generalife terraces and against the luminous background of the Mountains of the Sun (Sierra Nevada).

But, if the Alhambra was white, why was it called "the Red Palace"? The most widely accepted version is that of Ibn al-Jatib, who justified the name by reference to the glow given out by the torches used to illuminate the hasty, night-time construction of the walls. To the Muslims living in the plain, the building must have looked a splendid red and so was termed 'al-Hamra', the Red. However, we should remember that Ibn al-Jatib was one of the greatest poets of his day and that his version is perhaps too appealing to be true.

Note the almost invariable use of the term Muslim rather than Arab when we speak of the former inhabitants of the al-Hamra. The word "Arab" implies, to some extent, a nationality, and the creators of this wonderful artefact that we call the Alhambra were Iberians, the grandchildren and great-grandchildren of earlier settlers of the Peninsula, who spoke Arabic and practised the religion of Islam, whose culture was the unequalled product of a glorious synergy of races. To conclude the introduction to this chapter on the Alhambra, let us consider the following words that the Almería poet F. Villaespesa dedicated to the Alhambra and which can be read on a plaque located beside the Puerta de las Granadas:

"When not even the shadows of these walls remain, their memory will endure for ever, as a unique refuge of Dreams and of Art. Then the last nightingale to grace the world will make his nest and sing his song, his farewell, among the glorious ruins of the Alhambra".

The Alhambra is the most important medieval Islamic citadel in the Western world. It housed an estimated 2000 inhabitants with all the facilities required by a combined city/palace. What has survived to modern times is merely the nucleus of what used to be.
The complex, today, can be divided into three parts: the Nasrid Palaces, the Alcazaba and the Generalife.

THE NASRID PALACES (or former Royal Palaces) may be divided into three : El Mexuar, the Comares Palace and the Court of the Lions.

THE MEXUAR ("await") was where the Council met, and also included administration offices.

THE COMARES PALACE included the Court of the Myrtles and the Throne Room, the official centre of the Alhambra.

THE COURT OF THE LIONS contained all the elements pertaining to private life, such as the harem, though it was also used in a political role, such as for receptions.

The Nasrid Palaces (below) are the main attraction for visitors and so are subject to the time restrictions marked on the entrance ticket.

Nasrid Palaces

Alcazaba

THE ALCAZABA is the silent embryo of what was to become the entire aristocratic city known as Madina al-Hamra (city of Alhambra).

It appears in History during the civil wars of the 9th century and in the struggles against the Almoravid and Almohad invaders, receiving various denominations, such as Elvira Fortress and Granada Castle, until from the 13th century the definitive name of Qa'lat al-Hamra (Red Castle) became established. For a long time, and even after the arrival in Granada of Muhammad ben Nasr Al-Ahmar in 1238, the founder of the dynasty, the Alcazaba was an independent fortress, separated by a deep gully from the plateau to the East (where the Nasrid Palaces were later constructed). In the times of Yusuf I (1333-54) a line of walls and watchtowers was raised over this gully. The remains of the walls can be seen today in the Plaza de los Aljibes, near the Puerta del Vino.

The Alcazaba (left) *was a military area of which there only remains a double wall and vestiges of military installations.*

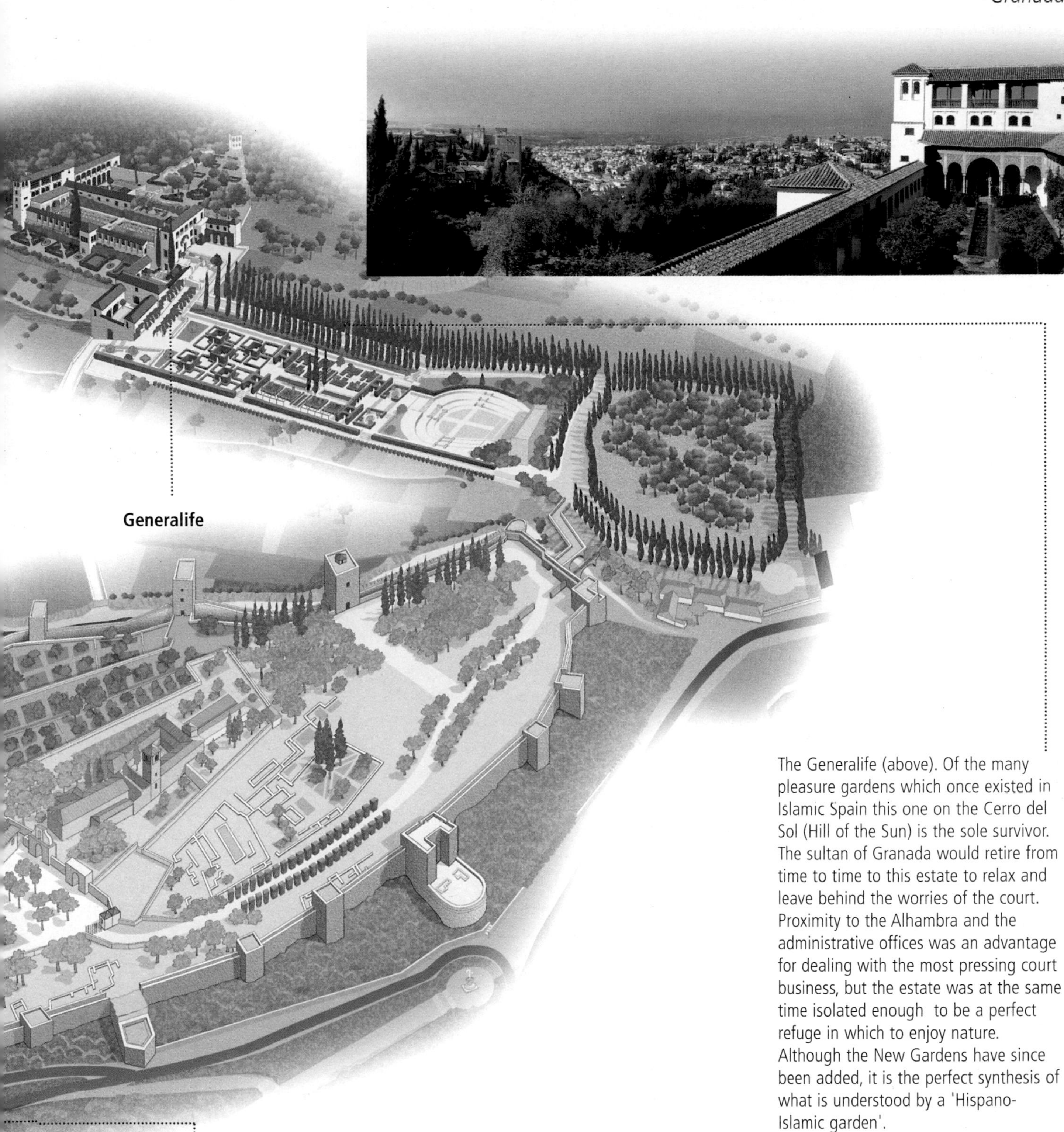

The Generalife (above). Of the many pleasure gardens which once existed in Islamic Spain this one on the Cerro del Sol (Hill of the Sun) is the sole survivor. The sultan of Granada would retire from time to time to this estate to relax and leave behind the worries of the court. Proximity to the Alhambra and the administrative offices was an advantage for dealing with the most pressing court business, but the estate was at the same time isolated enough to be a perfect refuge in which to enjoy nature. Although the New Gardens have since been added, it is the perfect synthesis of what is understood by a 'Hispano-Islamic garden'.

After the Christian conquest the emperor Charles V decided to build a new Renaissance imperial palace alongside the old Nasrid palaces, but due to political and economic difficulties (such as the Morisco war) it was never finished.
Its imposing bulk seems to dominate all around, but it was never meant to compete with the Nasrid palaces and in fact the architect, Pedro Machuca respected the older buildings in his plans.

THE ALCAZABA

Looking west and down from the top of the Watch Tower two distinct enclosures can be seen, one within the other. Sandstone blocks in the lower part of the walls of the smaller, or inner, enclosure suggest that it is of Roman origin. These original buildings were reconstructed in 889 during the Caliphate when the Alcazaba was being defended against the mozarabs and muladies of Umar Ben Hafsun.

For a very long time, and even after the arrival in Granada of Muhammad Ibn Nasr al-Ahmar in 1238, the Alcazaba was an independent fortress, separated from the flat land to the east (where the Nasrid palaces would be built) by a deep gully. Over this, in the reign of Yusuf I (1333-54), a line of walls and towers was built, remains of which can still be seen in the Plaza de los Aljibes. The same sultan connected the Alcazaba with the royal palaces by building a stout wall with a battlemented protected walkway on top to ease communication between the two.

It seems likely that the Watch Tower (27m. high and 16m. broad) was built by Muhammad Ibn Nasr al-Ahmar (1238-73) founder of the Nasrid dynasty. All four floors have suffered many changes by being adapted over the years to living accomodation. The tower is somewhat lower now having lost its battlements in several disasters starting in the 16th century. The first was the earthquake of 1522, then came the explosion of a gunpowder store in the Darro valley in 1599 which left it cracked and weakened and then in 1882 a flash of lightening destroyed the belfry which had to be rebuilt in a different position. The bell was cast in 1733, replacing an earlier one, and serves to regulate irrigation times in the Vega.

From this superb vantage point the view to the north is of the ancient Albaizin district and towards the north-east of the gypsy quarter of El Sacromonte, still waiting for long promised conservation aid. Above it is the Hermitage of the Archangel Michael and running down from here the old city walls of Granada, full of history and ancient scars.

In the Spring the Albaizin, whose murmurings and throbbings reach the tower top even over the traffic noise, seems enveloped in the scent of flowers so distinctive and inseparable from the characteristic houses, that it pervades the memory even when far away.

The hill of the Albaizin is separated from the Alhambra by the Darro valley which extends to the right to the Valparaíso (Paradise Valley) replete with the smells and scents of strawberries and quiet waters. This is the Granada that Gautier called "a celestial Jerusalem" and which the Cordoban al-Saqundi described as "pasture for the eyes and rapture for the soul". To the west spreads the modern city, as inhuman as any other. To the south is the hill of Mauror with the Vermilion Towers on top.This is an ancient fortress which defended the military camps here and the dungeons scattered about the hill. In the far distance, where earth meets sky, is the hill called 'The Last Sigh of the Moor', and the peaks of the Sierra Nevada mountain range, which are covered with snow for most of the year. The iron-coloured foothills are dotted with pretty white villages with evocative names. Nearer, to the east is the stony grandeur of the Charles V Palace, and beyond, at the foot of the Cerro del Sol, is the Generalife, "gardens without equal", whose cypresses, "solemnly stretch heavenward beseeching peace and solitude for the gardens".

Directly below the tower on the western side is a military construction in the shape of a conical cap with the tip turned down towards the Darro river. This is a 15th century artillery emplacement and, tellingly, faces the city. It forms the real 'prow' of the Alcazaba. It would seem that the governors of the Alhambra feared the inhabitants of Granada more than they did enemies from outside. It was for this reason that the Christian kings preferred to instal themselves in the Alhambra rather than in the old fortress in the Albaizin which had become enclosed by the accretions of new houses and from where a quick escape would have been difficult. The Alhambra, in contrast, was never encircled in this way and although much building work and alteration had to be carried out, it offered ready means of escape to open country if flight became necessary.

The Alhambra always remained outside the city walls of Granada. From the south side of the emplacement descended a wall with a walkway on top for the guard and which crossed over the Bab Handac (Gate of the Gully) demolished in 1526 to make way for

the Puerta de las Granadas (Gate of the Pomegranates). The walls, strung with forts and towers, continued down to the city to enclose it completely.

The Puerta de las Armas (Arms Gate) was the main entrance to the Alcazaba and had a portcullis controlled from the floor above. The gate was reached from the Alcazaba via the ramparts walkway. This gate-tower is attached to the bailey of the Alcazaba and adjacent to the Watch Tower.

A visitor going up from here to the royal palaces (whether on horseback or on foot) would have to travel some 90m. with his right side unprotected from the crossbowmen on the inner wall (the shield of course, was carried on the left arm). After passing another control point in the Torre de la Tahona (Bakery Tower), the remains of which can still be seen, the visitor arrived at the 'zoco' or market. Just before the tower, on the right a short climb led him to the Plaza de Armas (Arms Square) divided by a central street with small houses for officers of the garrison on either side,as well as workshops for black-smiths, armourers and so on and, at the end, was a bath for the soldiers. Parts of all of these still remain above ground. There are also water cisterns and a dungeon which has the sleeping area of each prisoner maked out in brickwork. Apart from the Watch Tower the square is enclosed by the following towers: Tower and Gate of Arms, de Alquiza, del Criado del Doctor Ortíz (of Dr. Ortiz's servant) and in the north-east corner the Torre del Homenaje (Homage Tower)which is almost as high as the Watch Tower.The Homage Tower, dating from the period of the Caliphate, is one of the oldest of the Alcazaba. Archaeological evi-dence based on the different construction materials suggests that the base might date from the 9th century and that al-Ahmar rebuilt his tower on top. Next along is the Torre Quebrada (Cracked Tower), consolidated to the level of the walls, has two floors and is so called from the enormous crack, best seen from the Plaza de los Aljibes, which ressem-bles a cut running from head to foot.

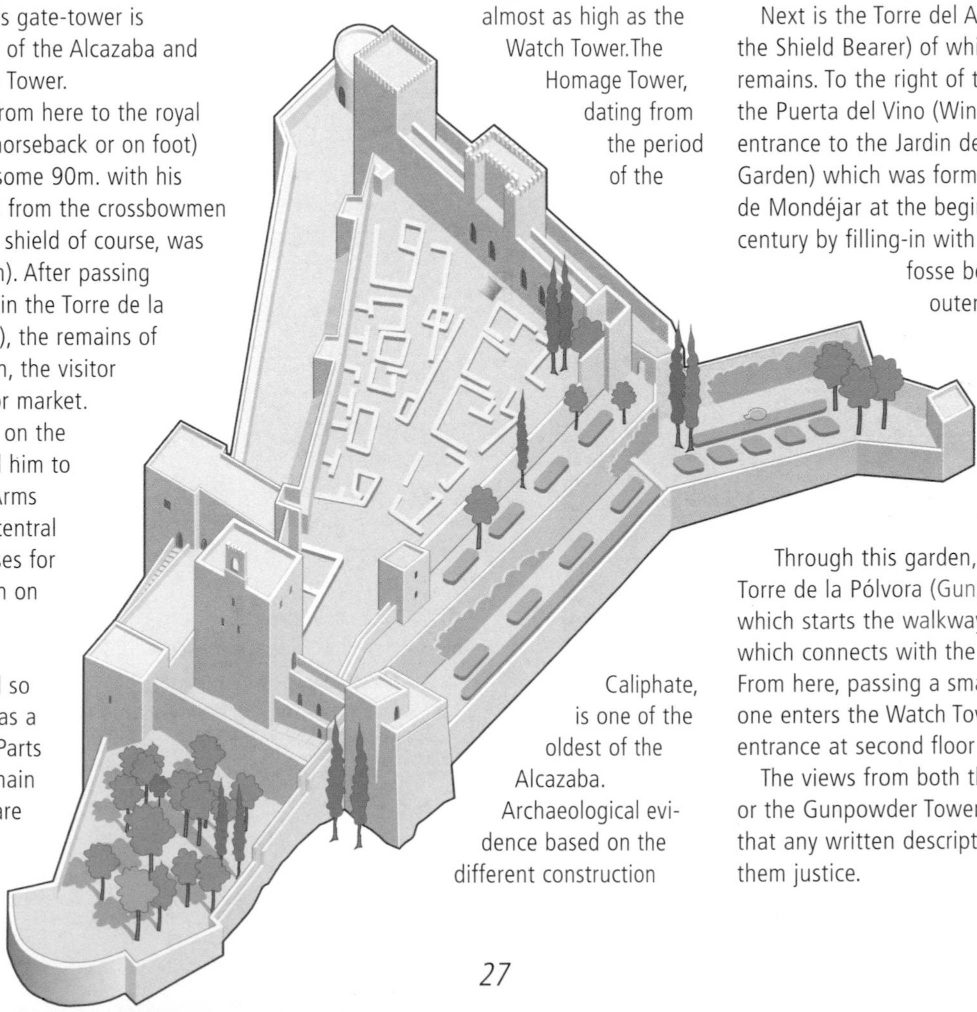

Next is the Torre del Adarguero (Tower of the Shield Bearer) of which only the shell remains. To the right of this tower, opposite the Puerta del Vino (Wine Gate) is the entrance to the Jardin del Adarve (Ramparts Garden) which was formed by the Marqués de Mondéjar at the beginning of the 17th century by filling-in with rubble the deep fosse between the inner and outer walls. Along the inner wall were two towers of which only the Torre de la Sultana (Sultana's Tower) remains.

Through this garden, to the east, is the Torre de la Pólvora (Gunpowder Tower) from which starts the walkway for the guard and which connects with the Vermilion Towers. From here, passing a small un-named tower one enters the Watch Tower by a modern entrance at second floor level.

The views from both the Ramparts Garden or the Gunpowder Tower are so spectacular that any written description would fail to do them justice.

THE MEXUAR

This is without doubt the part of the Nasrid palaces that has suffered most alteration, mostly carried out for the sovereign by the Christian governor, and adapting the layout to new uses and functions. The Hall of the Mexuar is perhaps the oldest remaining part of the royal palaces, although it was much reformed during the reigns of Yusuf I and his son Muhammad V (14th cent.). After the Christian conquest a chapel was installed in the hall, but it was found to be too small and so was enlarged by knocking down the north wall to make room for the choir, of which only the wooden balustrade remains today. The large windows are also a Christian addition as is the ceiling which replaced a lantern roof supported by the four central columns. This lantern had windows on its four sides to let natural light into the hall through coloured glass . At the end is a much restored Muslim oratory.

Sala del Mexuar

The Court of the Mexuar

This courtyard used to be wrongly called 'The Court of the Mosque'. On the north side is the Cuarto Dorado (Golden Room) and opposite, the imposing façade of the entrance to the Comares Palace. In the centre of the courtyard is a carved white marble fountain, a copy of the original. The portico of the Golden Room (left) is formed of three finely proportioned arches supported on slim columns crowned by capitals, also of marble, which might be Almohad (12th. or 13th cent.). Behind the gallery is the Golden Room with a gothic window divided into two lights by a mullion and opening on to the woods. Most of the work is Christian but the ceiling is original, although redecorated with gothic motifs.

Patio del Mexuar, galería Norte.

THE COMARES FAÇADE *(right and opposite)*. For many the beauty of the façade on the south side of the courtyard is beyond description. Oleg Grabar asserts, "...this façade appears curiosly out of place, too large and too formal to be a mere passageway...". On a frieze on the façade is the following inscription, 'My place is that of a crown and my entrance a parting of the ways; the Occident believes that in me is the Orient...'. The façade stands on a plinth of three white marble steps forming a sort of dais and the stucco decoration increases in complexity as it rises, perhaps in imitation of the classical orders. It finishes with wide and beautifully carved wooden eaves the rafters resting on a wooden frieze, and all carved to the same exquisite standard. Almost all authorities agree that these eaves are the masterpiece of Hispano-Islamic carpentry. Above the lintel of the doors are remains of the original tiling. The stucco decoration around the doors down to the dado of tiling is modern as is the dado itself. The aesthetic impression of this façade, wherever it may originally have been, must have been very moving, multicoloured as it was, like a Persian carpet , with the eaves gilded and the bronze doors burnished.

Fachada del Mexuar

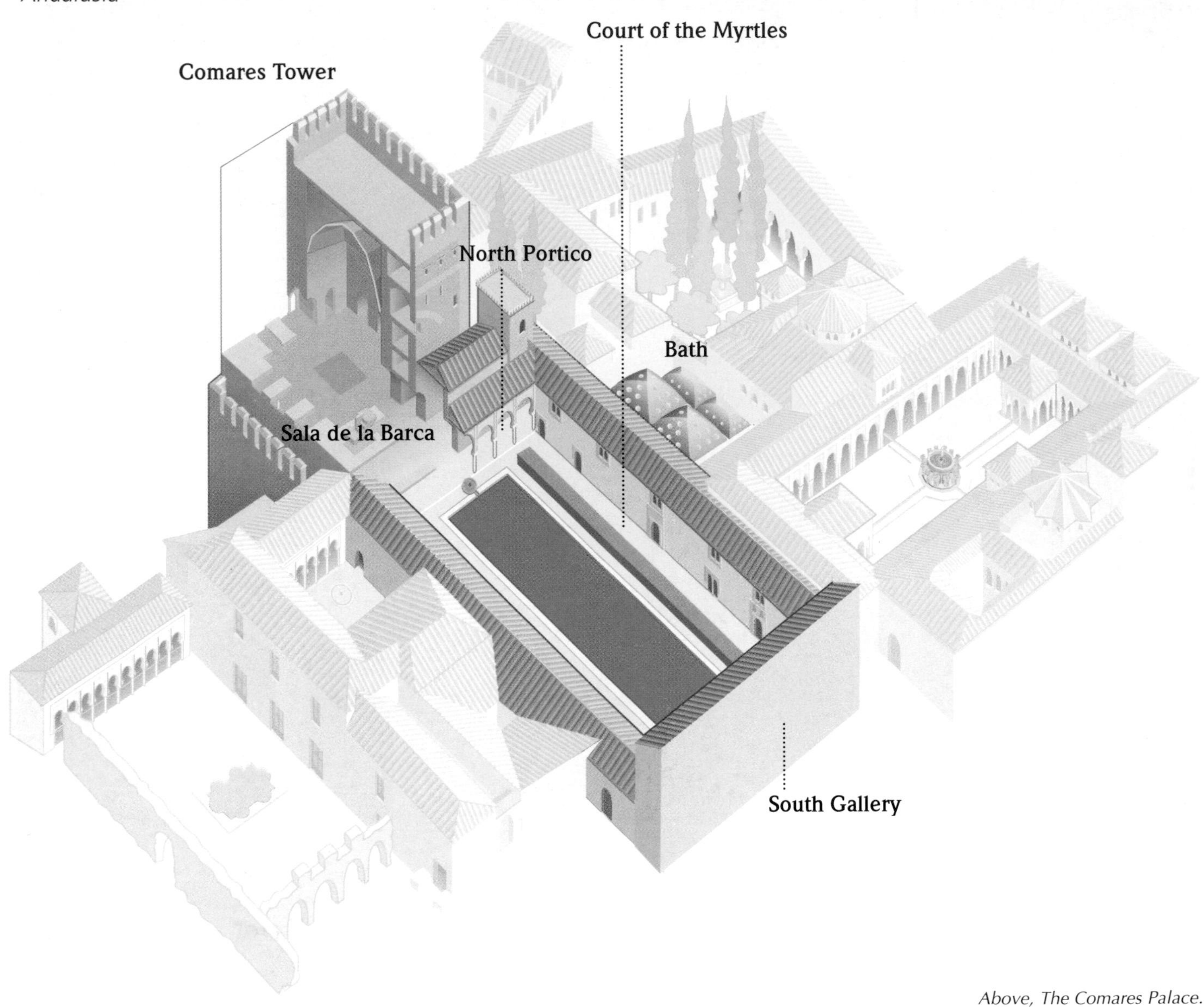

Above, The Comares Palace.
Opposite, Reflection of the tower in the pool.

THE COMARES PALACE

This palace, containing the Ambassadors' Hall or Throne Room, forms a nucleus which is the most important of all the buildings in the Alhambra. The austerity of its design and the balance of its proportions fill the court with such serene majesty that even now one seems to respire the noble grandeur of the sultans who built it.

The Court of the Myrtles was the centre of diplomatic and political activity in the Alhambra. It was almost certainly the setting for grand receptions given for foreign embassies, as well as being the place where important people would wait to be received by the sultan. Until recently the whole palace was attributed to Yusuf I, but it is now known that in those times the Court of the Myrtles was an open esplanade with a pool in the centre. It was Muhammad V (1354-96) who enclosed the esplanade to form a monumental court, although he did preserve the buildings of his father on the north side: the portico and Hall of the Boat, the Comares Tower with the Ambassadors' Hall inside and the palace bath.

The mediaeval visitor, having passed through the control at the main entrance, would walk in from the south and find himself before an enormous mirror of water, reflecting the white mass of the Comares Tower. The columns on the north side would appear to float on water

since the slope of the white marble pavement allowed the water to reach their bases. All the buildings on this side, including the tower itself, became as a floating palace, and thus, "while in the rest of Europe they built castles in the air, in Granada it was palaces on water". And this was because the prime function of the pool was that of a mirror, a conceit used again three hundred years later in the famous Taj Mahal at Agra (1630-47).

SALA DE LA BARCA. The Arabic greeting 'baraka' (a blessing) appears repeated in inscriptions all over this hall. It seems that a phonetic corruption of the word gave it its name, but the physical similarity of the ceiling to a small up-turned boat ('barca' in Spanish) reinforced the usage. In the jambs of the entrance arch to the hall are two beautifully carved niches of marble which would have contained jugs of water, perfumes or vases of flowers.Water was a common symbol of hospitality as reference to it in the verses carved around the niches show. The entrance to the adjacent Ambassadors' Hall is under a great arch.

THE AMBASSADORS' HALL is still magnificent even though now lacking the stained glass windows which were destroyed in the explo-

Left: The southern Portico. Above: Ambassadors' Hall.

sion of 1590. According to an inscription which runs along the top of the tiled dado in the central alcove on the north side, it was in this alcove that the sultan sat in state. The inscription reads. '...Yusuf chose me to be the throne of the kingdom'. From this position the sultan exercised a certain psychological superiority over his subjects, but they would also feel themselves under the fatherly eye of their religious, political and military chief.

The ceiling is a masterpiece of native carpenters' craft. It is made up of 8,017 cedar-wood pieces in relief, forming seven symmetrical bands which terminate in the centre of the dome in a small honeycomb cupola. The design is a clear allusion to the seven heavens of Islam and is directly inspired by the Qur'an, and the tradition of the Prophet's journey to the heavens mounted on a white stallion and accompanied by the archangel Gabriel. High up, just below the cornice supporting this splendid ceiling are five windows on each side of the hall reminiscent of the architecture of the desert. The inscriptions in cufic, Maghrebie and Andalusian-cursive characters, are predominately of a pious nature and particularly noteworthy is the reiteration of the words, 'Allah alone is the victor', although there are also eulogies on Yusuf I. One of the inscriptions, scarcely visible on a capital in one of the alcove arches, reveals the public nature of the hall. Beseeching brevity, it reads:

'speak few words and you will leave in peace'.

THE COURT OF THE LIONS

This was the hub of the private quarters of the sultan and had rooms given up to the women of the court. It cannot be called the harem because it was not dedicated exclusively to things feminine, but was also used for diplomatic and political activity. It is now known that before 30th December,1362 the only building here was the Sala de Dos Hermanas (Hall of Two Sisters) and that the others which enclose the court are posterior. On entering the court its beauties slowly and progressively unfolded whichever of the paths round the colonnaded cloister was chosen. A forest of golden columns opened up before the visitor, to whom, slowly walking along, they would seem, "the golden fringe of a spread of lace suspended from the sky". The cause of this impression of weightlessness were the garden plants growing in the middle of the court, which blocked a view of the bases of the columns. The cubic capitals, originally multicoloured , support stilted arches with a lintel structure above. From the soffits of the arches hang delicate stucco 'curtains' which serve no structural purpose and are mere decoration. Above the lintel are the carved wooden eaves, the rafters also exquisitely carved, and all originally multicoloured.The great width of the eaves was intended to protect the arches and

columns.The uniformity of the capitals and columns is only illusory since there is a great diversity of decoration not apparent at first sight. On the east and west sides are pavilions projecting into the court. Each has a small fountain and beautiful wooden domed ceilings which still retain some of the original multicolour. These perfect domes are constructed with flat pieces of wood. In the centre of the court the Fountain of the Lions refreshes the air, spouting water from the mouths of twelve white marble lions which, standing in an outward facing circle, watch over all parts of the court. Some think that the whole fountain might once have been multicoloured, and there are indications that some of the sculpture has been scraped. Coming in from the Court of the Myrtles the first room encountered is the Sala de los Mocárabes and the nearest to the original entrance.The name comes from the original honeycomb ceiling of which only fragments survived the explosion of 1590. The present plaster ceiling dates from the 17th century. From here and going round the court in an anti-clockwise direction the Sala de los Abencerrajes is on the right. The hall is named after the Abencerrajes, a powerful local clan.

They were the political rivals of another powerful family, the Zenetes, who according to legend, hatched a plot to involve one of the Abencerrajes in an amorous adventure with the sultana. They succeeded in exciting the jealousy of the sultan with the result that thirty-six Abencerraje knights were murdered in this very hall. This popular story leaves it unclear as to which sultan was resposible, but tradition has it that the iron oxide marks in the bed of the fountain are the bloodstains of those killed. Between the two entrance arches, and on leaving, there is a corridor which leads to a staircase to the upper floor where, in all probability, the ladies of the palace lived with their younger children.On the same floor is the Patio del Yanan, in which are conserved remains of mural paintings and black marble capitals.

La Sala de los Reyes (Hall of the Sultans)

This occupies the whole east end of the Court of the Lions. It is divided into five spaces, three of them lit by the great arches giving on to the court and separated from the other two which are in shadow. Set into the springers of the honeycomb vaulting which covers each one of these spaces, are twenty windows with lattice-like screens of plaster, and at each end of the hall are alcoves at right angles to the long side.

From the alcove on the south side, the hall displays a succession of spaces of light and

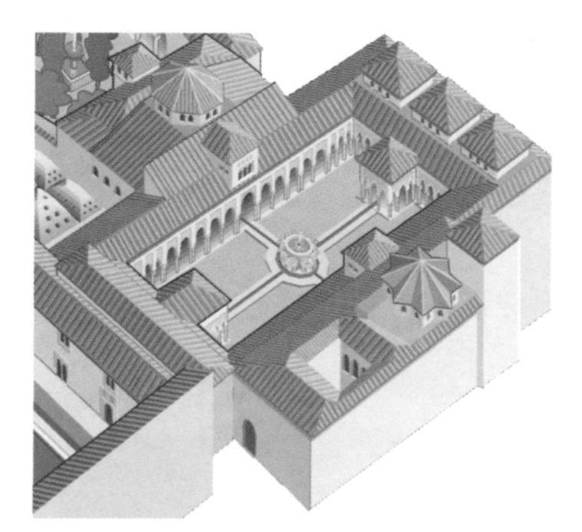

shadow defined by great pointed plaster arches, each one decorated differently.This variety of decoration and the play of light and shadow means that what might otherwise tire the eye, as elaborate and repetitive baroque decoration does, is instead a pleasure and the Ideal of the modern interior designer, " a sense of harmony between different features", is achieved. In the ceilings of the alcoves along the back of the hall are paintings realized on sheep-skin and fixed to the wooden ribs of the vault with glue and bamboo pegs. This system of pegs and glue prevented potential damage from rusting nails and also the loosening of the paintings due to differential shrinkage and expansion of the pegs and the ribs. The central alcove, the grandest of all, was no doubt reserved for the sultan, his intimates and important guests. Seated within, the scene seems an oasis seen through a clump of palm trees with the Fountain of the Lions in the middle. Painted on the ceiling of this alcove are personages who are traditionally thought to be the first ten sultans of the dynasty. It is generally accepted that the paintings on these ceilings date from the end of the 14th century or beginning of the 15th. The paintings in the other two alcolves seem to share certain

themes. Two personages, one Christian and the other Muslim, perform various feats to win the favour of a Christian lady. The story ends in the southern alcove, where the Muslim knight spears his Christian rival before the entreating gesture of the lady, who is watching the tournament from a tower. Most experts agree that the paintings show a clear Tuscan influence.

La Sala de Dos Hermanas (Hall of Two Sisters). In spite of what was formerly believed, it is now known that this hall is the oldest of the buildings around the Court of Lions. As with all the other rooms of the court, the original name of the hall is not known, the present one being merely descriptive, the two 'sisters'

Left: Cupola of the Sala de los Abencerrajes. Above: Cupola of the Hall of Two Sisters.

being the great slabs of marble from Macael on either side of the central fountain. The dado of coloured tiles is perhaps the most beautiful and the pattern the most original in all the Alhambra. Above the dado, in Andalusian-cursive script , and running right round the room is a lovely *qasida* by Ibn Zamrak. It uses the metaphor of a garden to describe the beauty of the room, and the exquisiteness of the honeycomb cupola above, a miracle of craftsmanship made up of over five thousand separate pieces. The square plan of the hall (8 x 8m.) turns, high up, into octagonal by means of sqinches filled with honeycomb decoration. Above is another octagonal with twin windows set in each side which throw natural light on to the honeycomb cupola and until 1590 were glazed with coloured glass. A verse from Ibn Zamrak's *qasida* sums up the aesthetic impression the hall produces;'In this place will the soul fall into a reverie'.

El Mirador de Lindaraja Beyond the Sala de los Ajimeces, an elongated hall with windows to left and right and a honeycomb ceiling, is the wonderful Mirador de Lindaraja. The name appears to come from a corruption of three Arabic words; 'ain-dar-Aixa', that is; 'the eyes of the house of Ayesha ('mirador' is a lookout). It is possible that once building work on the Court of the Lions and the Court of the Myrtles had been finished, Muhammad V reverted to using the Ambassadors' Hall and reserved the Hall of Two Sisters as a residence for the sultana (dar al-Malika) and the royal family. In the north side of the mirador is a graceful double window giving on to the Lindaraja garden . The window ledges around retain their original height. Before the Christian gallery was built enclosing the garden, there would have been a view from this window over the walls to the city beyond. Above, crowning the mirador, is a skylight with coloured glass set in a wooden lattice, flooding this tiny room, with coloured light.Here a delightful day might be spent seated on cushions on the floor. Around the window is a lovely verse, 'In this garden I am an eye full of joy, the pupil of this eye is, in truth, my lord'.

The dado here is made up of tiny ceramic chips and in the jambs of the arch are narrow panels with exquisite inscriptions picked out in black on a white background alluding to Muhammad V. They are the finest and most intricate in the palace.

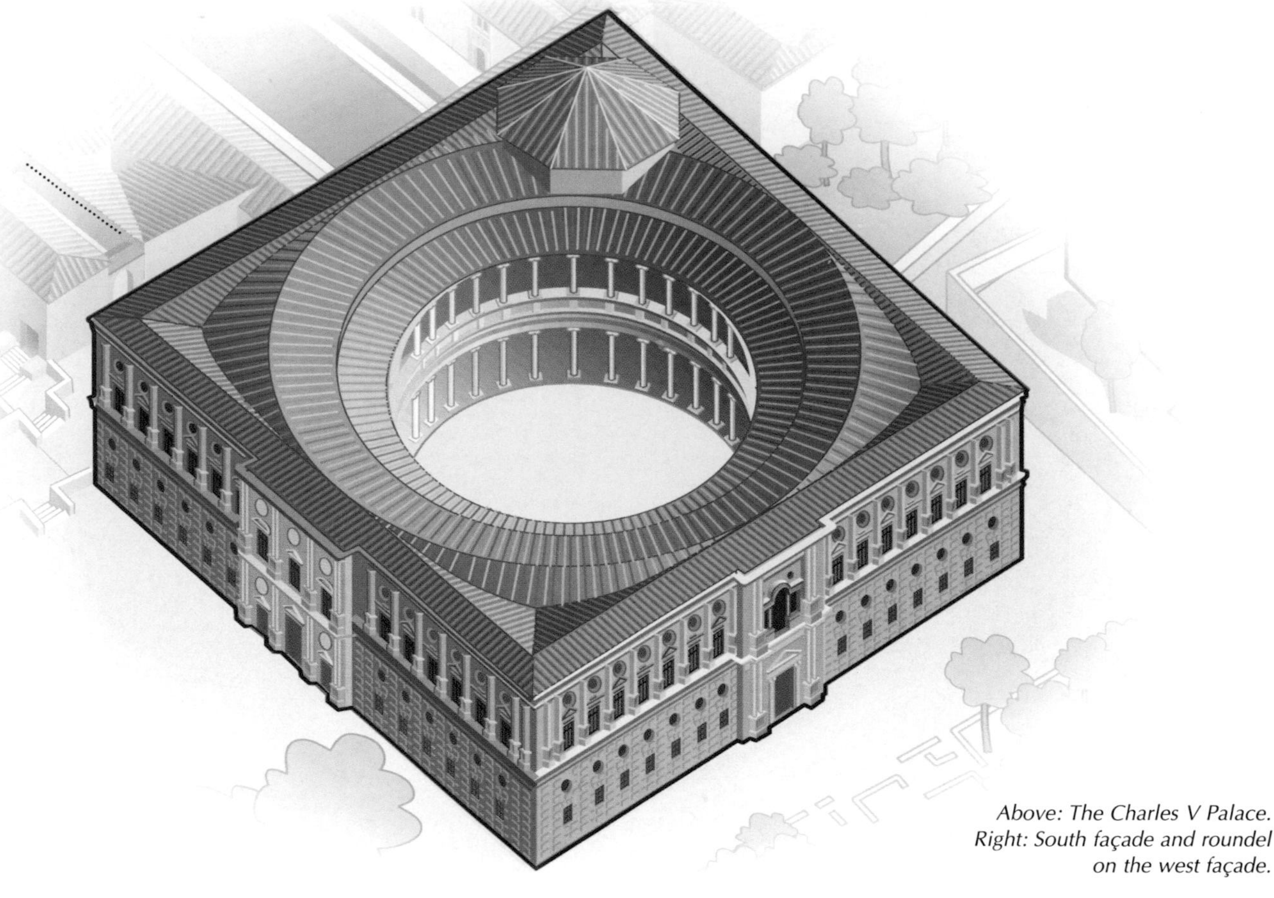

Above: The Charles V Palace.
Right: South façade and roundel on the west façade.

THE CHARLES V PALACE

No monumental building is so controversial, misunderstood and yet so often cited as outstanding, as the Charles V Palace. This arises in part from ancient prejudices and a profound ignorance of the role Granada played in the grand schemes of the 16th century Spanish monarchy. One might say that the view so dear to 19th century romantic travellers, of an idillic Muslim world swept away by fanatical Spanish monarchs is still held to some extent. The true story is rather different. Nowadays all historians understand the value as a symbol that the Spanish monarchy gave to the conquest of Granada.

It was decided to convert a centuries old Muslim capital into a truly splendid and symbolic Christian capital, by encouraging a flood of Spanish and Italian artists and architects to Granada.There existed, therefore, a political will to re-enforce, with grand royal buildings, the status of Granada as the great capital it had always been. Bearing in mind that the Catholic Monarchs had already chosen Granada for their royal chapel and mausoleum, it is understandable that their grandson, the emperor, should identify with their ideals and, as the arbiter of the destiny of Europe, personally seek to expand them. The result of all this was the emperor's order to the Marqués de Mondéjar, governor of the Alhambra and trusted advisor, to build the Charles V Palace. This person, vital in the history of the palace, came from one of the great Spanish noble families, the Mendozas. Many members of the family had been educated in Italy and, beginning in Toledo, did much to disseminate Renassaince

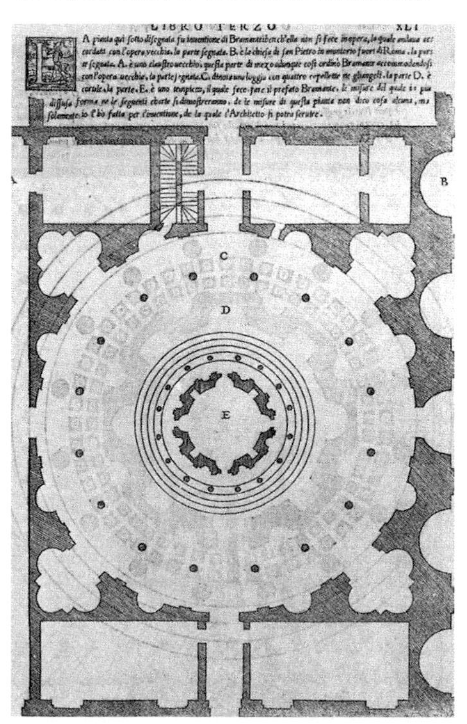
LIBRO TERZO XLI

LA pianta qui sotto disegnata fu inventione di Bramante ... la parte segnata. B. è la chiesa di san Pietro in montorio fuori di Roma ... la parte D. è ... la parte. E. è uno tempietto, il quale fece fare il prefato Bramante ... solamente io l'ho fatta per l'inventione, de la quale l'Architetto si potra servire.

art throughout Spain. His commission to Pedro de Machuca, the architect of the palace, to design the Charles V Fountain at the entrance to the Nasrid castle shows that Mondéjar was a true Renaissance man.

The influence of Renaissance ideas was felt in Andalusia more strongly than anywhere else outside Italy, and this is due to the contrary nature of two cities: Seville, which was the centre of trade with the Americas, and Granada, a capital symbolic of centuries of strife with the Islamic world. The building of the Charles V Palace was not an isolated event, but yet one more beat in the pulsing new world order evolving in Andalusia.

And what is, in fact, the meaning of the palace ? It has been accurately defined as the symbol of a kingdom started in a hurry and never concluded (the roof of the palace, it should be noted, is modern). It was a tax on the Moriscos that financed the work but this brought two problems: in the first place these taxes had previously been spent on hospitals and welfare and it was felt incongrous that a Christian emperor should use it for his own palace. The second problem was the rebellion of the Moriscos, a particularly cruel civil war, which ruined the kingdom of Granada (one might say for ever) stopped the taxes and left the palace unfinished.

Pedro Machuca, the architect of the work, had been trained in Italy and worked with Michelangelo and Raphael.Thanks to this he was completely up to date on the latest ideas and theories of the Renaissance. A proof of this is his choice of a singular ground plan, a circu-

lar court within a square, achieving a perfect form aspired to since the days of the architect Alberti. Precedents can be found from San Piero in Montorio in Rome, which was to be ringed by a circular court according to the plan drawn by Serlio, to the circular court of Raphael's Villa Madama or the drawings of palaces by Leonardo. The original designs, now in the library of the Royal Palace in Madrid, included esplanades in front of the south and west façades, but these were never constructed. The circular court has a diameter of 42m. and great salons along the sides with the exception of the bevelled-off corner in the northeast which is a chapel and crypt. The chapel was of especial interest to Charles, and on receiving the plans on 30th November, 1527, he wrote to the governor; "I wish only to tell you that the front hall should be big and that there should be a chapel to say and hear mass".

In this original plan the palace was already conceived as an extension to the Nasrid palaces. Machuca was in charge of the work until his death in 1550. He was succeeded first by his son Luis and then by Juan de Orea, who worked under Juan de Herrera, doing the staircase and the upper part of the principal façade, which was then finished off by Juan de Minjares.The interior is sober, with two storeys in Doric and Tuscan Orders and a grand principal staircase, the stairwell covered by a round ceiling. And all so competently woven together by Machuca's sure touch that every stone block is a marvel of precision.

Running right round the façade is a marble bench, above which are two storeys. The first is rusticated after Italian precedents and stresses the horizontality and weight of the building. The second has Ionic pilasters with delicately carved reliefs, and by contrast emphasises lightness and verticality. Both storeys have round and rectangular windows, the play of lines and shapes being very much in Renaissance taste.

Of particular interest are the sculptures which are symbolic and allegorical references to the emperor as Caesar. So too, from classical mythology, he is compared to Hercules in the reliefs of the principal façade by the Italian sculptor Niccolao da Corte recording the battle of Mülberg. The female personages in the sculptures on the south front are Fame, Victory and Fertility, and are the work of da Corte, Juan de Orea and Antonio de Leval. These scuptures identify and make visual the Imperial Concerns clearly stated from the Hill of the Alhambra to the conquered city below.

The palace was built over a Christian quarter attached to the Nasrid palaces. The minimal damage done to the Nasrid palaces was due to a geometrical error and such an ambitious and innovative project as the Charles V Palace would certainly not have been allowed had it radically affected the old palaces. It is probably thanks to the emperor's palace that the Alhambra was incorporated into the Crown Estate rather than being left a crumbling ruin recalling a lost culture.

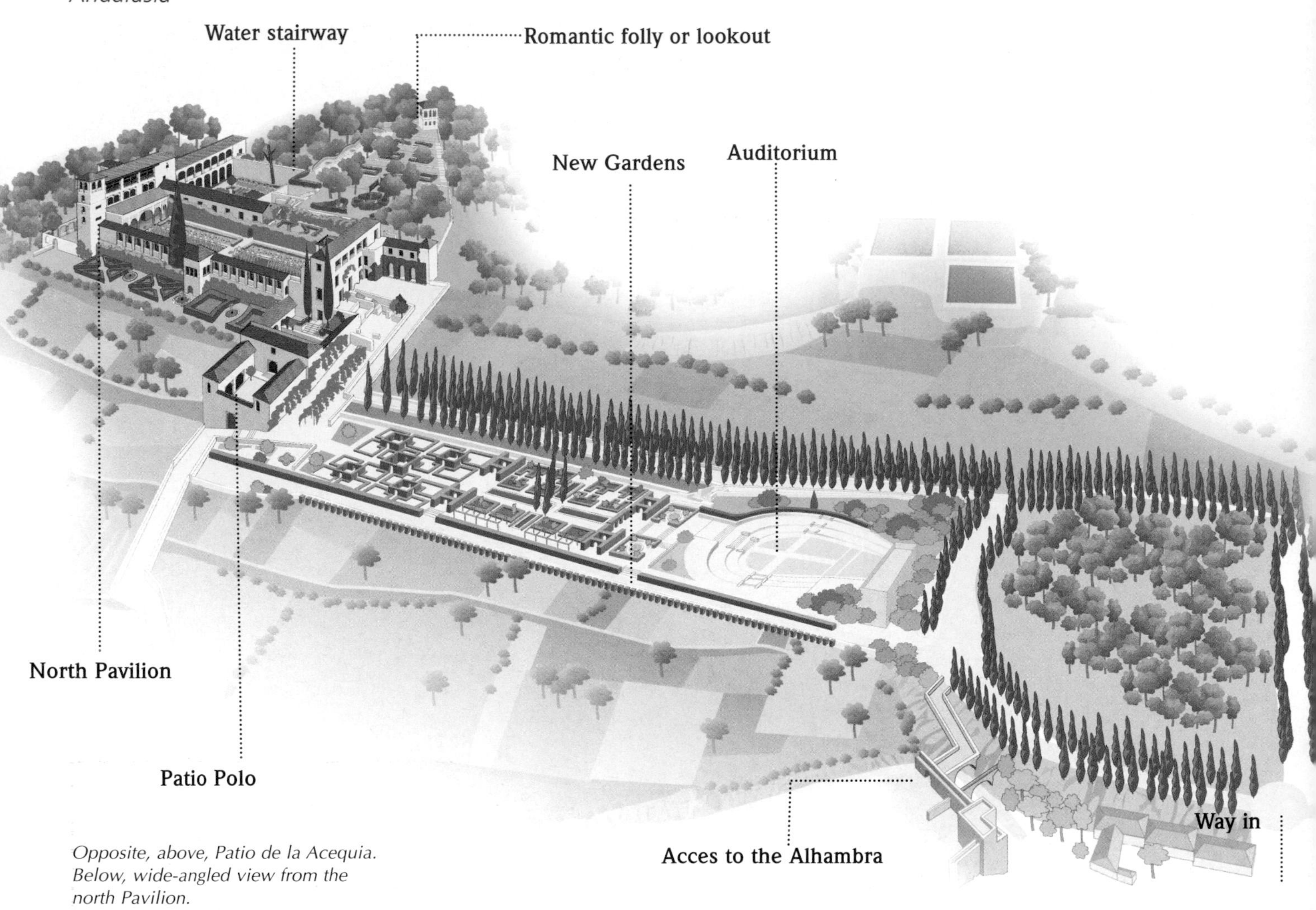

Opposite, above, Patio de la Acequia. Below, wide-angled view from the north Pavilion.

THE GENERALIFE

According to most authorities the name Generalife is derived from two Arabic words: 'djennat'; that is garden, orchard, paradise and so on, and 'al-Arif'; architect or builder. The most probable meaning then, is `Garden of the Architect´, although some, referring to contemporary Muslim and Christian authors, translate it as, 'first among gardens', or 'the most high and noble of gardens'.

An important source of information on how the Generalife used to work is found in Ibn Luyun's, 'Tract on Agriculture'which dates from the 14th century. He writes: "For a house among gardens a site ought to be chosen on a height for security.It should be south-facing and close to the entrance to the estate. A well should be dug or a water tank installed on the highest point, but better is a water channel running through the shade of the plants and trees. Close-by, the beds will be planted with great variety so as to be green and pleasant to the eye all year round, and a little further off will be beds of assorted flowers and evergreen shrubs and trees. An extended vineyard will run right round the gardens and in the centre the vines will cover with shade the paths crossing the beds. In the middle will be a pavilion for times of repose, surrounded by climbing roses, myrtles and other flower varieties used to embellish a garden. The house should be longer than it is broad so as not to tire the eye, and in the lower part have a room for the owner's guests. Hidden among the trees will be a pool. It would also be useful to built a dovecote and a small, habitable tower. For the protection and peace of mind of the occupants, the house ought to have two doors.".

All that is left of the original gardens are the hanging terraces, still cultivated. These terraces rose to the top of the hill in such a manner that looking down on them they appeared to be one single slope, covered with the colours of flowers and fruit trees. The modern gardens bear no relation to those of the Middle Ages when flowers and fruit trees were mixed together. For the Muslim of the age there was beauty in a pepper or an artichoke. Modern gardening plays only with the senses of smell and sight, but a Muslim garden was designed to be enjoyed for its display of flowers, their scent, for the sound of water, and for the pleasure of eating the fruit while strolling under the trees.

All these characteristics are found in what is left of the residence about the so-called Patio de la Acequia,(´water channel`) but so altered that for example, the mirror effect the pool would have had in Nasrid times, is lost. Originally the water would have poured gently into the pool from the little fountains at each end, making a low murmuring sound like soft music which would not disturb the mind. During the reign of the Catholic Monarchs, the high west wall was lowered and arches opened in it. They did leave the lookout in the middle, which was the only opening in the wall in Muslim Times. The north face, the best preserved, has five round horse-shoe arches, the central one being higher and wider and behind are three more, similar, arches. These give on to a narrow room at right angles to the pool, which has a decorated wooden ceiling. It is the antechamber to a lookout which is slightly out of line, towards the right, with respect to the long axis. Five small windows open above the aforementioned three arches and the fact that a poem inscribed around them refers to sultan Abu-l-Walid Ismail and mentions the, 'year of the great triumph of Islam', fixes the date of the

THE CHAPEL ROYAL

The Conquest of Granada was a great triumph for the Christian world, threatened in the East by the Turks. The creation of this Chapel, from its conception during the lifetime of the Catholic Monarchs, Ferdinand and Isabel, as the place where they would be buried, symbolized the Christian victory, the culmination of a secular dream successful due to steadfast human will and, above all, to Divine Providence. The Queen expressed this explicitly in her testament: "My wish and command is that my body be buried in the city of Granada" and the royal decree of 1504 stated that the chapel was to be constructed beside the Cathedral. Building work, under the direction of Egas, advanced so rapidly that in 1521 the bodies of Ferdinand and Isabel were brought down, in a solemn procession, from their provisional grave in the Alhambra. The Chapel building above the tombs, like others in their respective kingdoms, was built in the Gothic style of the period, following the Franciscan convent model, with a few peculiarities due to the special purposes of the building. It is a dynastic funerary chapel intended to form part of a larger complex, and thus segregated, but not to the extent of creating a private, family space, due to the symbolism that transcended the Monarchs themselves. This is why the Crypt is Franciscan in its simplicity, the Queen being a devout follower of this Order to the extent that she was buried in her Franciscan habit, because "in death, we are all equal". Nevertheless, the role of the Crown was

to be made quite clear, and is ever-present in all its regal splendour: thus, the retable of the High Altar (by Vigarny) with its pyramidal hierarchy from God Almighty down to the martyrdom of St. John, the patron of the family, to the mortal figures of the King and Queen at prayer and the historical events represented on the second socle of the altarpiece (to the left is the surrender of the city to Ferdinand and Isabel).

Like its own historical circumstances, the construction of the Chapel reflected the conjunction of two periods and two mentalities. The Gothic, spiritual and stylized, seeking the heights and idealizing the forms, in contrast to the Renaissance, the "new Roman style", which is present in the Carrara marble sepulchres *(right),* sculpted in Italy by Domenico Alessandro Fancelli and Bartolomé Ordoñez, the illustrious pupil of Michelangelo. The new style rediscovers clasical nudes and the sensuous movement of Mannerist forms, affirming that man is the centre and measure of the new Universe. It is decorated with Laocoöns and mythological creatures, half beast, half human, together with faun-like angels around the coats of arms, providing a link to the images of the classical world. The grille *(below),* that divides the chapel in two was forged by the master Bartolomé de Jaén in the early 16th century with gilded embossed iron, the most important work of its kind of the century.

Opposite top, the Catholic Monarchs. Opposite below, iron grille by Bartolomé de Jaen. On this page, the royal tombs

n the Sacristy, as well as personal objects of great historical value in display cases, such as the Queen's sceptre and crown, Fernando's sword with its gold hilt, Isabel's casket and missal, there is also a variety of liturgical vestments and the cloths for the campaign altar that accompanied the Monarchs on their march towards the city.

But what is most impressive, perhaps, for its intrinsic value, is the collection of Flemish panel paintings that belonged to Queen Isabel of Castille. Although much depleted, it is still considered the principal private collection and it exercised a great influence on Spanish art. Isabel's father, don Juan II, was an enthusiast of this novel pictorial style and Jan van Eyck is known to have visited the Court during a journey to Portugal. The fact that commercial relations between Castille and Flanders were based on the export of wool explains why the most important non-religious painting, of the Arnolfini Marriage in London, should come from Ávila. The wedding of Juana to Philip the Handsome was also the occasion of new additions to the collection, many of which are now on display in the Prado Museum. The importance of these paintings is such that further comment is justified: the early Flemish painters did not invent oil painting but it was they who explored its possibilities and discovered a new outlet. Paintings in tempera dried very quickly and so the traditional mixture was replaced by another with drying oil and a novel substance that was soluble in oil yet did not produce an emulsion. The new formula dried much more slowly and this allowed the artist to create transparent colours that could be applied in layers, superimposing areas of veiling and thus highlighting the most luminous parts and achieving much brighter and more dynamic colours than ever before, allowing the light to reflect off the smooth, opaque background. The Italians had discovered the third dimension with the aid of the visual pyramid and now the Flemings took the opposite route; they achieved the illusion of reality by patiently adding one detail after another until they obtained a painting that was a kind of mirror of the visible world. Perspective, rather than being the basis of form and proportion, was limited to the secondary, technical role of unification. The structure created was surrounded by a space that was infinite, immaterial, intangible but ever-present; it seemed to exude from objects and then to expand limitlessly. In other words, this space did not determine the forms or fix the proportions that defined them, but was rather something ethereal that enveloped and surpassed everything.

Such a space is tempered by the light that gives reality to forms and to the objects that it seems to emerge from. Only painting in oils enables these atmospheric lighting effects to be reproduced, the relationship between the infinitely small and the universe considered as a whole, the perfect union between the space within and that beyond the frame of the picture. This new Flemish realism, moreover, developed a hidden symbolism according to which everyday objects were imbued with symbolic meanings disguised under the aspect of the visible world. In the Chapel we can enjoy the work of Rogier van der Weyden, van Eyck's successor, in two parts of a triptych showing the Nativity and the Descent from the Cross. In the latter, all degrees of suffering are nobly restrained, without resorting to exalted or unnatural gestures. The lines and the colour reflect the artist's own feelings; the colours are light-toned, with the volumes scarcely distinguished and the contours diffuse, although the outlines of the nose, eyebrows, lips and face are painstakingly detailed. In the Nativity, Mary's hands are elegant and aristocratic, slightly accented by the chiaroscuro that moulds the forms emerging into the progressive clarity of the light. This artist is a painter of spirituality.

From Dieric Bouts, we have the triptych that presides the Sacristy *(above)* and some portraits *(left)*. He is considered a worthy successor to van Eyck, 'the inventor of landscape', due to his sharp eye for space and the relations between the characters and the landscape, from which he removes all superfluous detail to achieve his austere, mystic and profoundly religious world. With Hans Memlinc and his exquisitely sensitive portraits, we enter the world of Dutch religious painting, whose influence extends to the 19th century.

THE CARTHUSIAN MONASTERY. The Carthusians is a monastic order founded by St Bruno about 900 years ago, one of the various reform movements that took place during a period of crisis as a reaction against the power and spiritual deterioration of the Cluny monks. The most significant innovations were silence, isolation and fasting, all perfectly regulated to avoid physical and emotional disturbance. All Carthusian monasteries have the same structure, being divided into the church on one side and the two cloisters on the other after the confiscation of Church assets in 1835, the cells and the great Cloister disappeared, leaving just the church and the small Cloister, around which we can see, today, the Refectory, two chapels and the Chapter House. The unique feature of this monastery is to be found in the two parts of the church, the Sacristy and the Sagrario or Tabernacle, where Andalusian baroque achieves its peak of expression. The building comprising the church, of Herrerian sternness outside, is the cell of Jesus, the first hermit, the guest of honour, and thus must be decorated in an exceptional way. Moreover, it is the heart of the community life, where the monks spend up to 8 hours a day at prayer. As usual, it is made up of three parts: a choir for lay brothers by the entrance, separated by a screen with glass-panelled doors from the second choir, for monks, and from the Presbytery which, in this case, is divided into the High Altar and the Tabernacle or Sancta Sanctorum. It was in this small space where Hurtado Izquierdo succeeded in recreating in marble and gold the post-Tridentine notion of the exaltation of the Eucharist. This, however, can only be a figurative representation in stone, the work of man, and thus limited and merely symbolic of what will be eternal glory.

The central temple or great Sacrarium, destined to receive the body of Christ, is the source from which all life springs, and so this doctrinal concept is materialized as the double spring with seashells (the symbol of water-life), from which Divine Grace flows. The celestial dome that crowns the temple (by Palomino) contains the well-known Renaissance symbol in which the Holy Trinity presides the birth of the Universe, a theme which was also adopted in the Baroque. In this case, the figures of the Holy Fathers, the Angels, the Virtues and the Evangelists at the base of the dome, as they are at the base of all faith, all revolve around St Bruno who holds up the terrestrial globe and its heavy burden of Humanity's sins, over which, triumphantly, arises the Eucharist.

The adjoining Sacristy is considered by many to be the last great work of Spanish Baroque. This monastic chamber, far from being just one more within the monastery is, in fact, the most important of all after the church itself, and is where the monks prepare for the most important part of the day: the communal Mass. This is the antechamber to the sacred occasion, and is itself sacred, reminding us of a small church distinguished by the marquetry work of the vestment drawers, inlaid with marble, silver, mahogany, tortoise-shell, lotuswood, ebony, etc., created over 34 years by brother Vázquez, expressing his devotion by his handiwork. For the diaphanous paving, Hurtado Izquierdo used two-coloured rhombuses that open in all directions to draw attention to the pilasters and walls, covered in intricate and varied patterns of white stucco, creating a space that is transparent and luminous.

Left above, tryptic by Dierec Bouts in the Sacristy of the Chapel Royal. Left, Portrait of Christ by the same artist.

Above the Sacristy and a drawing of the Monastery

THE CATHEDRAL

The masterpiece of the Spanish Renaissance, it reflects like no other the splendid moment of Spanish imperial history when Carlos V dominated Europe and, above all, it reflects the genius of the greatest architect of the century: Diego de Siloé, from Burgundy. After conquering the city from the Moors, a great church was needed for the newly Christian city, to proclaim the triumph of the Faith. A project similar to that of Toledo cathedral had been prepared, but when Siloé took charge in 1528, he personally visited Carlos V to convince him of the desirability of adopting the new "Roman" style, deemed to be more appropriate for an emperor. Siloé was familiar with the innovations introduced by Brunelleschi and Alberti in Italy, but he had his own ideas for the great cathedral with which to develop the full range of his genius. He discarded all the earlier construction work and, starting from fresh foundations, constructed an apse and amblatory both of which were absolutely innovative and revolutionary. These two solutions of Siloé created a new school, and the model was repeated with variations in all the cathedrals to be built in Andalusia (Jaén, Málaga, Úbeda, Guadix, Cádiz, etc.). His influence outlived the centuries and even crossed the seas, as many South American cathedrals owe him a great debt. The apse *(above right)* is a prodigy of skill and imagination, combining a triumphal arch 30m. high with a dome that is 45m. high and 20m. wide. For the columns, as well as a high plinth, he "reinvented" the superimposition of orders, which was a novel solution in the Renaissance. By these means, when the height of the architrave was reached, the central aisle was raised by another 15m. with a second group of pilasters. The result is spectacular in terms of spaciousness, lumi nosity and volume. It is not a church that invites absorption but is rather the expression of an ideology, the exponent of a historical moment, that at the same time is laden with religious content. The apse, designed to be a cenotaph, is dark at the base, as is the world of man himself, but rises towards the brilliant light of the stained glass windows, towards the heavens illuminated by the Passion of Christ which may only be reached through the Virgin Mary, whose life story is reflected in the transitional paintings between the two spaces. All this is sustained by columns bearing the Apostles, and in particular the four Evangelists, the true pillars of the Faith who `support´ the whole weight of the toric arch. Of Siloe´s many followers, outstanding is Alonso Can[illegible]on-structed the great fa[illegible] the triple triumphal arch, according to the directions of the original plans, though adding his own touch of genius to create a completely baroque style.

Cano is also the painter whose work depicting the life of the Virgin graces the first storey of the marvel that is the apse. Cano, too, is the author of the statue of the Virgin Mary in the Sacristy, a masterpiece of baroque sculpture in which the overwhelming majesty of the mother [illegible] God does not contradict her soft, delicately innocent expression.

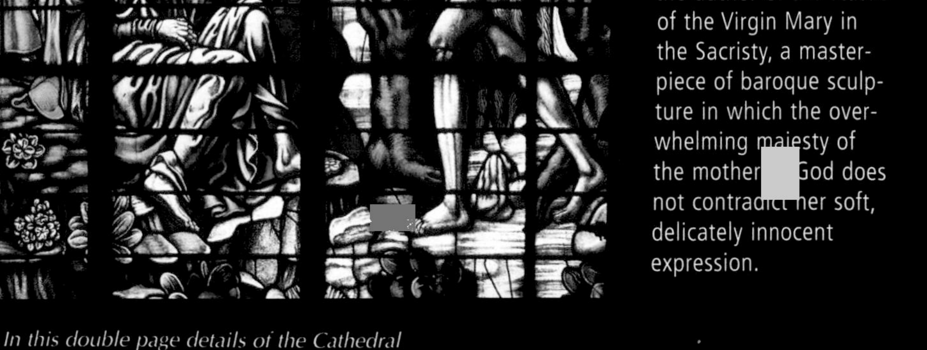

In this double page details of the Cathedral

Left, Montefrio. Above Guadix and below la Calahorra

Left, Moclin. Below Salobreña and Capileira

Huéscar
Villanueva de las Torres
Freila
Benalúa
Lugros
Guadix
Huéneja
Moclin
Laroles
Chauchina
GRANADA
Fuante Vaqueros
Santa Fé
Capileira
Pampaneira
Trevélez
Loja
Lerín
Bubión
Órgira
Sorvilán
Motril
Salobreña
Almuñecar

The contrasts in the province are so strong that in 40 km. one goes from an alpine climate to the tropics. The terraces of the Alpujarras form the steps from the white of the mountain peaks, down the green slopes, to the blue sub-tropical sea. Towards the North-West, where snow may also be seen, there is desert land at Gorafe-Guadix, while the North is characterized by mountains and olive plantations.

SEVILLE

Seville was founded and christened Hispalis by the Phoenicians approximately 28 centuries ago in the depression that formed the lower Guadalquivir, at a height of between 8 and 16 metres and about 100km from its mouth. The river has determined its history both positively and negatively: thanks to the fertility of the land, easy access to the river, and its strategic position overlooking the fertile Andalusian plains, it became a Tartessian centre and coveted Carthaginian colony which the Romans used as a theatre for their operations. Scipio founded Itálica in 205 AD over which Pompey and Caesar competed for control and where the emperors Trajan and Adrian were born. The Vandals, who gave the name to the entire region, conquered and destroyed it, and the Visigoths chose it as the base for their civil wars against Toledo in the 6th Century. This was in the era of the bishops Saint Leandro and Saint Isidoro. The

Muslims renamed it Yzvilia, and it played a dominant role in the first three centuries of Cordovan rule, but was left devastated by the Vikings (844) until it was converted into the most important independent Taifan kingdom (1023) aspiring to the inheritance of the Caliphate, eight years before the fall of Cordoba. Sultan al-Mutamid almost gained it but, under the Christian threat of Alfonso VI, asked for help from the Almoravids (1090) conscious that he was changing the course of the history of al-Andalus. Later, the Almohads arrived (1146), made Seville their capital and built the Giralda (1198). Fifty years later, the Christians led by Fernando III also chose it as their base. From 1504 to 1717, it held the commercial monopoly of the Americas, that is to say it was the major European city and commercial centre in the gold trade, and hence a cultural centre in its own right. Such a lineage has given it the particular heritage it has today.

April Fair in Seville

Patio of Casa de Pilatos

Town Hall

Museum de Bellas Artes (Fine Art)

Isla de la Cartuja

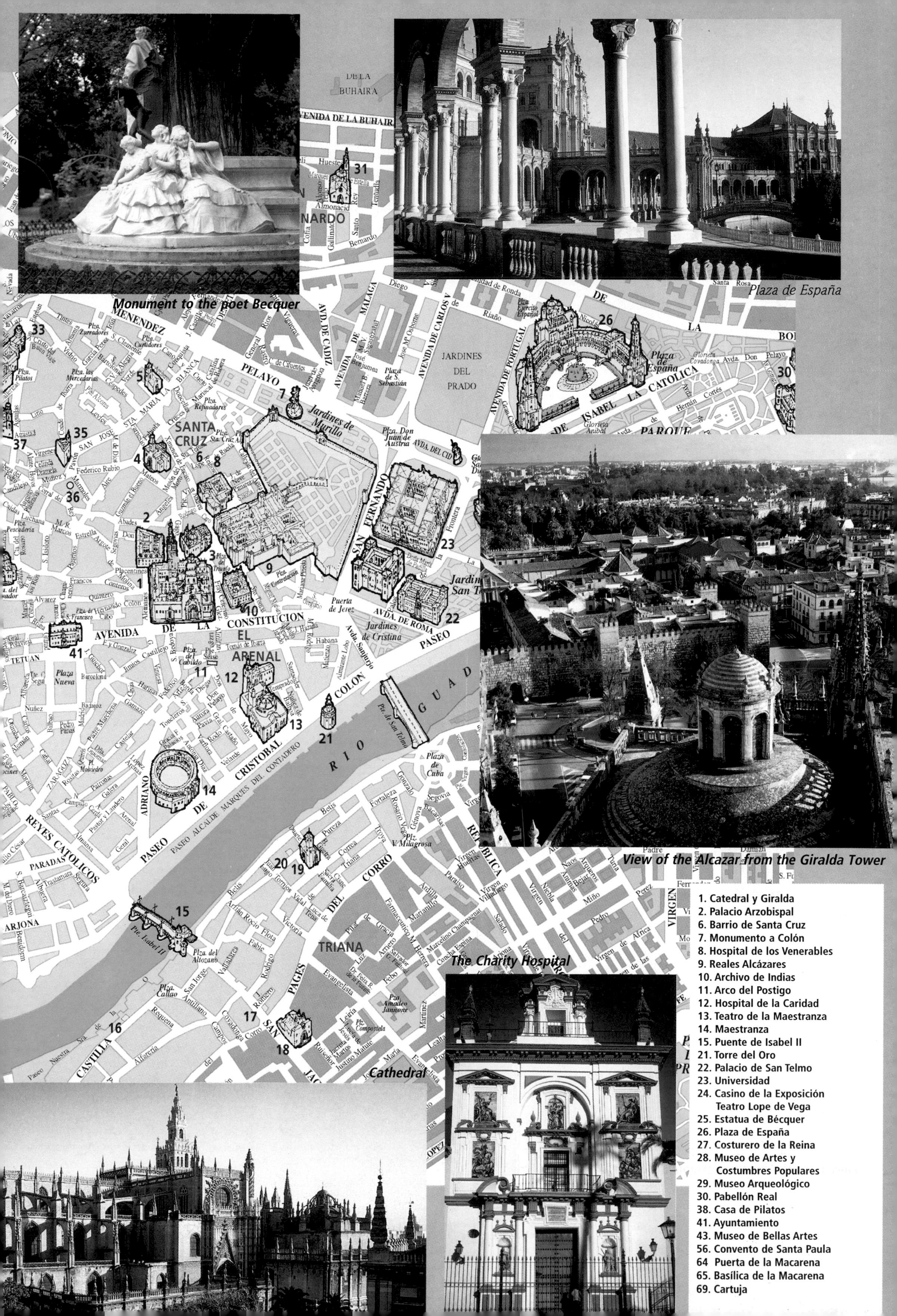

Monument to the poet Becquer

Plaza de España

View of the Alcazar from the Giralda Tower

The Charity Hospital

Cathedral

Above, Patio de las Muñecas. Right Patio de las Doncellas

THE ROYAL ALCÁZARES

Remains show that in the Roman era there already existed an important commercial and military seat based by the Guadalquivir, but it wasn't until the 9th century and the Taifa kingdoms that the Abbasid dynasty made it their major centre, linked to the Caliphate of al-Andalus. The invasions by the Almoravids and above all the Almohads (1146) provided open spaces, baths, porches, the large crossed stonework patios complete with fountains trees and flowers. This Almohad style spread throughout al-Andalus and eventually arrived, centuries later, in the Alhambra itself.

After the capture of the city in 1248, Alfonso X, known as "The Wise", built his Gothic palace and shortly afterwards made his mark on Seville and Toledo with the authentic and unique Spanish art known as Mudéjar, a synthesis of both cultures and styles in which Almohad decoration is incorporated within Christian Gothic design. The height of this understanding between the two cultures came with Don Pedro I de Castilla, known as The Cruel or The Avenger (1350-

This gate in the old wall opens onto the Patio de la Montería. In the background is the imposing facade of the palace of Pedro I (left) masterpiece of the Mudéjar style and a monument to tolerance. The work was carried out by craftsmen from Granada, Toledo and Seville. It served as the inspiration for the façade of the Comares Palace in the Alhambra which at that time (1365) was reaching it greatest splendour under Muhammad V, Pedro´s good friend.

were brought here from the ruins of Abderrahman´s palace in Cordoba by sultan al-Mutamid. Like Abderrahman, King Don Pedro himself also transformed his palace for his lover, María de Padilla.

The adjacent Patio de las Muñecas *(previous page)* is also organised around the central court but as a separate section with an intimate atmosphere. Its exquisite layout has survived the more recent restorations without losing its charm in spite of the increased height. The differently coloured columns don't

Above, the entrance to the Ambassadors´ Hall (Salón de Embajadores).

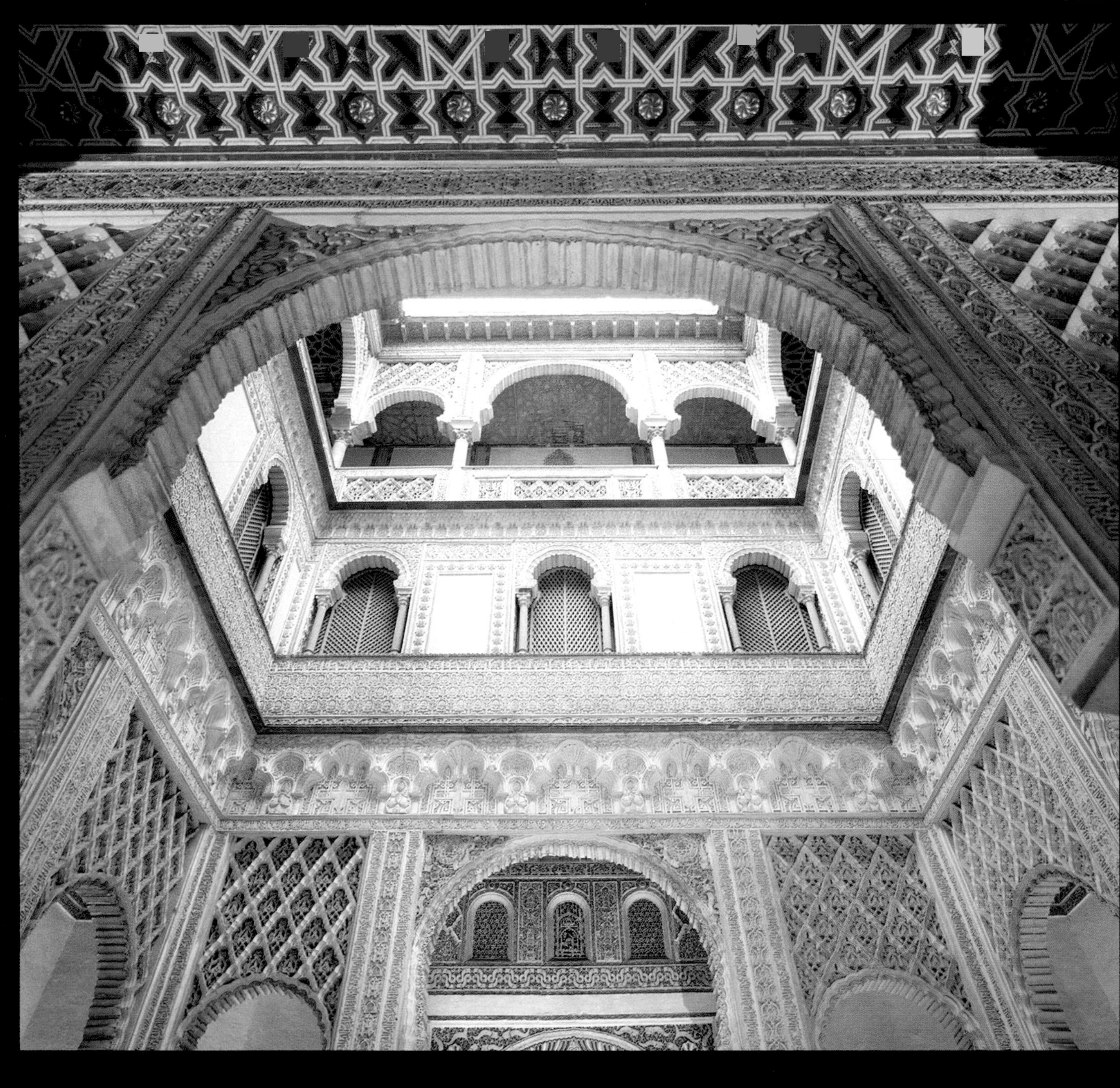

Above, two views of the Patio de Las Muñecas

quite seem to match the diverse capitals they support increasing the impression of fragility. However, the rhomboidal stucco-work decoration *(Sebka)* of Almohad origin gives it transparency and lightness. Also very prominent are the wooden carvings which cover the ceilings and doors of the Alcázares *(right)*. In general this work was carried out by Moorish carpenters, who were well experienced in Castilian churches and palaces. They easily adapted to any place or ideology because the predominance of geometric forms, which had such a significant religious importance for the Muslims, did not conflict with the Christian faith. The development of these styles gave rise to an almost unlimited variety of aesthetic forms. Each epoch and culture also left its particular mark on the gardens, which form an integral part of the complex. Also important is their role in relation to the surrounding buildings which they were designed to complement.

Below: Left, Fuente de Neptuno and Patio de las Doncellas

In this panoramic 180º view of the Ambassadors´ Hall you can see the cupola which gave its name to the Hall of the Half Orange (Salon de la Media Naranja) which extends outwards from a twelve-pointed star and is supported by honeycomb squinches which transform the square into a sphere. Once more the square symbolises the earth, and the golden cupola the celestial sphere in eternal orbit. Although the restoration was Christian it remains loyal to its original symbolism.

Above, the ornamental iron grille by Bartolomé de Jaen. Right, the interior of the Cathedral.

Above, Royal Chapel. Below, Crucifixion by J. M. Montañes and on the right, the vault of the Crossing

THE CATHEDRAL

After the conquest of the city in 1248, the old mosque was taken over as was customary, and for the following 153 years served as a cathedral. All that survives of this mosque are the Patio de los Naranjos and the Minaret (which is called the Giralda and is now the symbol of the city). The admiration of the conquerors for what they had captured didn't extend to the mosques, which were regularly "Christianized" or simply substituted by churches. This was also done with the old Romanesque churches. The geopolitical role of Seville in the 14th and 15th centuries, close to the sea and the Muslim kingdom of Granada, made Seville the nerve centre of the kingdom of Castile. The earthquake of 1366 gave rise to the construction of the third largest church in Christendom, so enormous was it that the builders declared, in their own words; "in the future we will be considered mad". Work began in 1401. The identity of the original architect is unknown due to a fire which destroyed the documents. The work, lasting more than a hundred years, was directed at the end of the century by masters such as Simon de Colonia, Alonso Rodríguez as well as the prolific Juan Gil de Hontañón.

The work which is in keeping with the late Gothic style was finally completed: the imposing verticality of the rhomboid pillars, which merge with the ribbed vaults, do not reduce with their dizzying height the sensation of spaciousness of the nave and four ailes, nor do they create spatial tension, but rather they enhance the diaphanous quality of the space itself. Due to the simplicity of the lines it may be considered a pure Gothic work, almost archaic. However, the passage of time has brought with it sufficient additions so as to form the most important and varied monument in Seville, in which every style and genre of work may be found. The first modification was made to the dome, which collapsed in 1511 and was replaced by Hontañón with the splendid ribbed,

starred vault which appears above. The altarpiece in the High Altar, the largest in Christendom (360 m^2) with forty-four relief decorations and more than a thousand figures relating to the life of Christ, also took a little more than a century before its first phase was completed, moving from the Gothic of Dancart to the Renaissance of Jorge Fernández (1525) before finally being covered with gold leaf by Alejo Fernández.

The main grille was worked by the finest master ironworker of the century; Bartolomé de Jaén and Brother Francisco de Salamanca (1518-1529). In the Choir the screen is also by Salamanca, there are one hundred and seventeen choir stalls and two magnificent High

Baroque style of organs by Duque Cornejo.

The Cathedral occupied the entire space of the old mosque except for the Patio of Ablutions *(left)* which gave it a monumental feel, with its nave and four ailes, side chapels, transept and apse which do not protrude past the outer walls. As a consequence there is a lack of directionality. There is no space to wander around (ambulatory) but only added spaces in which the chapels and sacristies are located. Buttresses and external flying buttresses were fixed to an ostentatiously carved block of stone, in place of the brick used by the Muslims, which was considered inferior.

The ROYAL CHAPEL, situated behind the High

Altar, houses the intact remains of St. Ferdinand in a silver Baroque casket as well as those of his son Alfonso X ("The Wise") and his wife Beatriz of Swabia. The Chapel is Renaissance work by Gainza (1551) although the dome is by Hernán Ruiz II of Cordoba (17th cent.). Here presides the altarpiece the Virgin of the Monarchs of great popular acclaim (13th cent.), product of French workshops and seemingly a gift to the Conqueror of Seville from his cousin St. Louis, King of France.

The importance of the cathedral chambers can be seen in the grandeur of its rooms, especially in the MAIN SACRISTY (1528-1543 AD.) with its Greek cross floor crowned with a half orange dome, the work of Riaño y Gainza, possibly with the help of Diego de Siloé. Among the paintings here are Campaña´s `Descent from the Cross´ and `St. Isidore and St. Leander´ by Murillo, as well as one of the best monstrances by Arce and the Alfonsine panels. The SACRISTY OF THE CÁLICES, of Gothic design (Alonso Rodríguez) is presided over by the paintings by Goya of St. Justa and St. Rufina, patron saints of the city. On the sacristy walls also hang other paintings; some by Valdés Leal, 'The Virgin with Child' by Zurbarán and a picture of St. John the Baptist, four panels by Alejo Fernández as well as the well-known painting of The Glory originally attributed to Tintoretto but which is now credited to Juan de Roelas, a talented Venecian painter.

The ANTECHAMBER and the CHAPTERHOUSE by Hernán Ruiz el Joven are of outstanding beauty with their domes and paving but equally amazing are the treasures that fill the chapels: The Chapel of The Virgin de la Antigua, patron of mariners, which also houses the sepulchre of Cardinal Mendoza de Domenico Fancelli. The world famous painting 'Vision de St. Anthony' by Murillo in the Baptismal Chapel was stolen but later recovered. In the Capilla de Scalas is the Virgin of Granada, from the della Robbia workshop. On the Altar of the Virgin of Bethlehem by Alonso Cano, we can see mother Mary with an unusually sweet expression. The Capilla de San Pedro still contains paintings by Zurbarán. The Chapterhouse and Colombina Library (with 90,000 volumes) also stand out amongst the Cathedral's treasures, which include donations from Alfonso X, The Book of Hours given by Isabel la Católica, and the 20,000 volumes donated by Hernando Columbus containing works and documents by his father, some in his own hand.

Above, Stained glass by Arnao de Vergara (1535 AD.) showing St. Sebastian with the figure of Carlos V. Below, Columbus' tomb (1891)

THE GIRALDA is one of the three great Almohad mosque towers (minarets) that still exist: the Kutubia in Marrakech, the Rabat tower, and the Giralda, although the latter wins out over her sisters in terms of grace and slenderness. It is also one of the few buildings of Muslim Spain in which the Christian intervention, far from distorting it, adopted it as the cathedral tower, giving it new value and symbolism. It was the minaret of the Mosque which was begun in 1184 . by Ibn Basso, with a base of solid stonework, and continued four years later in brick by Ali al-Gomari, until its completion with the Yamur, a spike with four balls, ten years later. The interior is made up of a series of small chambers with Almohad vaults and surrounded by the ascending ramp which lessens in both width and incline as it goes up. The earthquake that hit the Alcázar of Pedro I (1356) also brought down the Yamur, which was replaced in 1400 by a bell tower. It was Hernán Ruiz the younger (1558) who, in the middle of Renaissance work on the Cathedral, displayed an ingenious daring by adding the five parts which gradually decrease in height. The first and biggest is the Bells, followed by the Clock, the Stars, the Round, and the Crest. It all took ten years to construct

It is crowned by a colossal statue of Faith, `el Giraldillo´ a marvel of engineering which turns (Spanish: girar) like a weathercock with the wind. The statue gives its name to the tower. There is a copy inside the Cathedral.

Left, a romantic lithograph by Girault de Prangey from the middle of the 19th century. If we go by the sculptures on the High Altar of the Cathedral, this imaginary reconstruction by Girault seems very credible.

THE MARÍA LUISA PARK

Seville owes much of its charm to its welcoming parks and groves which fill the heart of the city, above all in spring, with their characteristic scent. The gardens of the Alcázar and those of Murillo were generously extended by princess Maria Luisa Fernanda who in 1893 donated half of her own garden which was adjacent to the Palace of Saint Telmo *(left)* to a city needful of more space, and in this way giving birth to the park which bears her name. In keeping with that era, the gardens, of French design, are romantic with a pastoral and nostalgic atmosphere. These days, they are a green and beneficial breath of fresh air in the centre of a city which is becoming more and more hectic and cosmopolitan every day.

Seville managed to secure the 1929 Latin American Exposition and was able to use this new space for the construction of the pavilions and buildings that would give a new look to the city centre. Don Anibal González

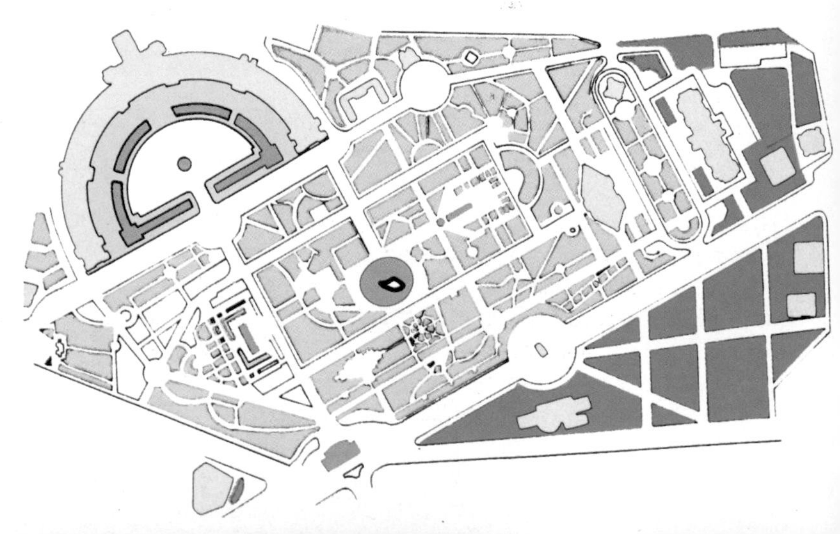

was the architect whose task it was to design the PLAZA DE AMÉRICA, in the southern part of the park, as the exposition's grand square of honour. To achieve this, he sought a synthesis of styles from the whole history of Seville, which ranged from Mudéjar to Neo-classical via Gothic, Plateresque, Flamboyant, Renaissance and Baroque, creating as a result the style known as Historicist Art or Traditional Regionalism. The square is organised around three pavilions: the MUDÉJAR PAVILION *(previous page above)* now the Folklore Museum, the ROYAL PAVILION, built of brick with ceramic cresting, and the PAVILION OF FINE ART, nowadays the Archaeological Museum *(above)*. Don Anibal González also designed the PLAZA DE ESPAÑA, the other large semicircular square surrounded by archways which was the central attraction of the 1929 Exposition *(overleaf)* surrounded by a lake and finished with glazed tiles, each referring to one of Spain's provinces. Today these buildings are used for public administration and central offices. Due to the Exposition, the Exposition Casino building and the TEATRO LOPE DE VEGA (Lope de Vega Theatre) were also erected. Over the years, the theatre has become too small, and has recently been replaced by Teatro de la Maestranza (the Maestranza Theatre) built not very far away for the other great twentieth century Exposition in Seville: Expo '92.

The Plaza de España

Although it is true that neither of the two twentieth century expositions fulfilled people's expectations for the city's development, Seville benefitted from the modernisation in terms of urbanisation and the transformation of its infrastructure which has provided it with advantageous conditions in order for it to achieve the hoped-for economic boom. In the same way that the old pavilions were turned into embassies, institutes, museums, cultural centres, etc, the modern intelligent buildings of the Island of Cartuja are moving in two clear directions: those of private enterprises which base their headquarters in the area which forms the Science and Technology Park in which the University takes part with the aim of boosting development; and the rest are geared towards the service sector with the Thematic Park as their centre, reusing the buildings that were the primary nucleus of Expo '92. Here the growing demand for multimedia and interactive entertainment using the latest technology is satisfied. In this sense, it also tends towards the so-called "Triana Cultural Gateway" which aims to mix culture and entertainment, a combination for which Seville has a historic vocation. Among the most positive consequences has been the restoration and rehabilitation of Cartuja de Santa María de las Cuevas, which was for a long time a ceramics factory.

On these two pages, there are pictures of the two twentieth century international expositions which left their mark on the city and have had strong cultural and historical influences on its heritage. Above left, the Mexican Pavilion in the Paseo de las Delicias, a mixture of native and colonial styles, with its intricate Andalusian-style grille which can be seen on the left. Previous page left, wooden lattice-work balcony in the Peruvian Pavilion and below, the Colombian Pavilion, both of which brilliantly encapsulate the amalgamation of cultures in which Seville played an important role. The two 180/ panoramic views are fine indicators of the Modern Age. Above, the Lago de España, the centre for aquatic shows, surrounded by the best in Spanish architecture at the end of the 20th century. Bottom left, the Avenida de Europa with its cooling towers.

BARRIO DE SANTA CRUZ (Santa Cruz Neighbourhood)

Although its reconstruction dates from the beginning of the twentieth century, it preserves the essence of Seville and its traditions like no other part of the city. It is also known as the JEWISH QUARTER, since it was in this area which surrounds the Alcázar that Fernando III and Alfonso X, above all, re-established the Hebrew community which had been expelled by the Muslims. The highest point of the Jewry was during the reign of D. Pedro I but they suffered under the persecution of 1391 and were expelled once and for all a century later, when their synagogues which had previously been mosques, were turned into churches.

The BARRIO, which keeps its secular structure is a true reflection of the of the history of urbanisation in Seville and Andalusia. The Muslims ignored the geometry of the Roman city and built their houses crammed together in Aljaimas around their mosques which were meeting points, in such a way that their whitewashed labyrinthine streets frequently lacked exits. They were very narrow in order to offer protection themselves from the summer sun. Each house was arranged around a coutyard with a fountain or well and plants. The squares, the parish churches, and open public spaces came afterwards with the Christian conquest. The neighbourhood of Santa Cruz is a mixture of both formulas: the patio, before intimate, now looked out through iron bars over the public street. Wandering through its streets you come across many surprises. One example being the Hospital de los Venerables, a refuge for destitute priests which was constructed at the end of the seventeenth century in the Baroque style

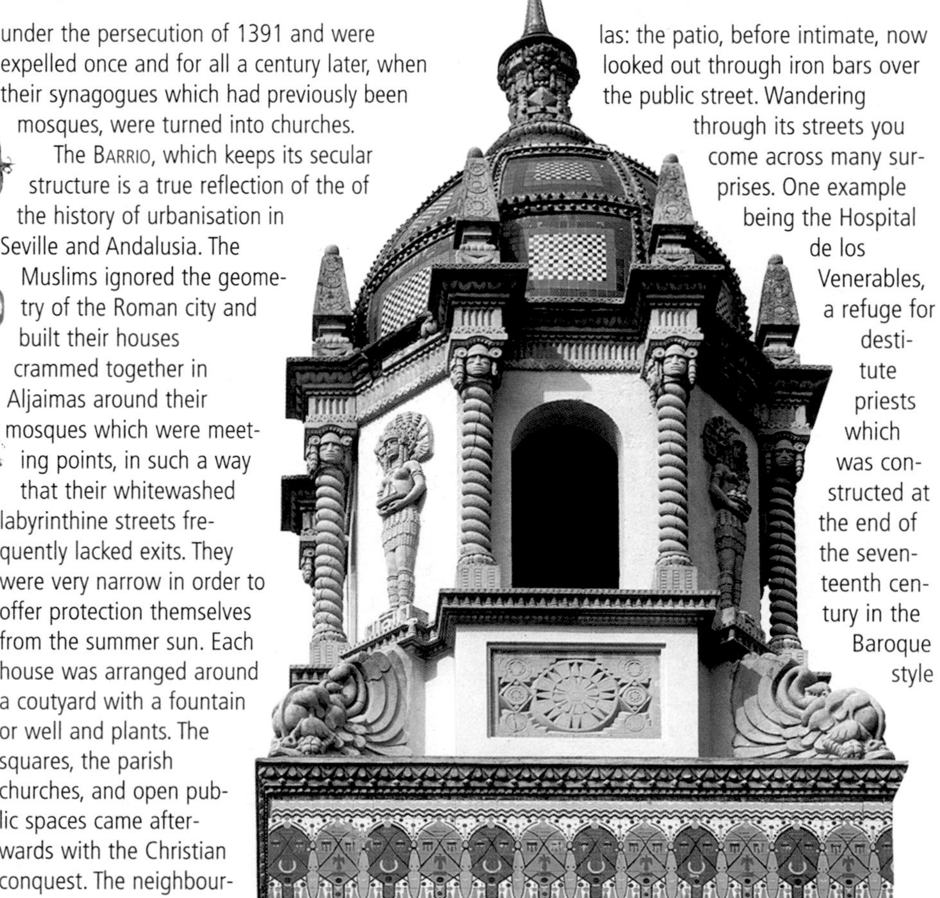

with a simple courtyard based on a play of line and an exuberant church which figures amongst the best of Andalusian Baroque with paintings by Valdés Leal. Nowadays it is a centre for exhibitions. Murillo also worked on this church and his House-Museum is just a few steps away. Another evocative corner is the CALLEJÓN DEL AGUA onto which looks the CALLE DE LA PIMIENTA. The most well-known part is the DOÑA ELVIRA COURTYARD (Plaza de Doña Elvira), planted with orange trees and with the Corral de Comedias nearby, where music can frequently be heard. The two-tone white and sandy orange break the brighter colours of the ceramics of the Trianera style workshop-stores. Other squares are the Alfero, scene of the opera Figaro, and that of SANTA CRUZ, with its magnificent 17th century wrought-iron cross *(left)*. In the plaza de los Refinadores proudly stands the statue of DON JUAN, famous inhabitant of Seville who inspired Moliére and Mozart among others *(right)*. The last outpost of the Jewry was in the neighbourhood of SAN BARTOLOMÉ, composed of multicoloured cottages and beautifully evocative streets such as Levíes.

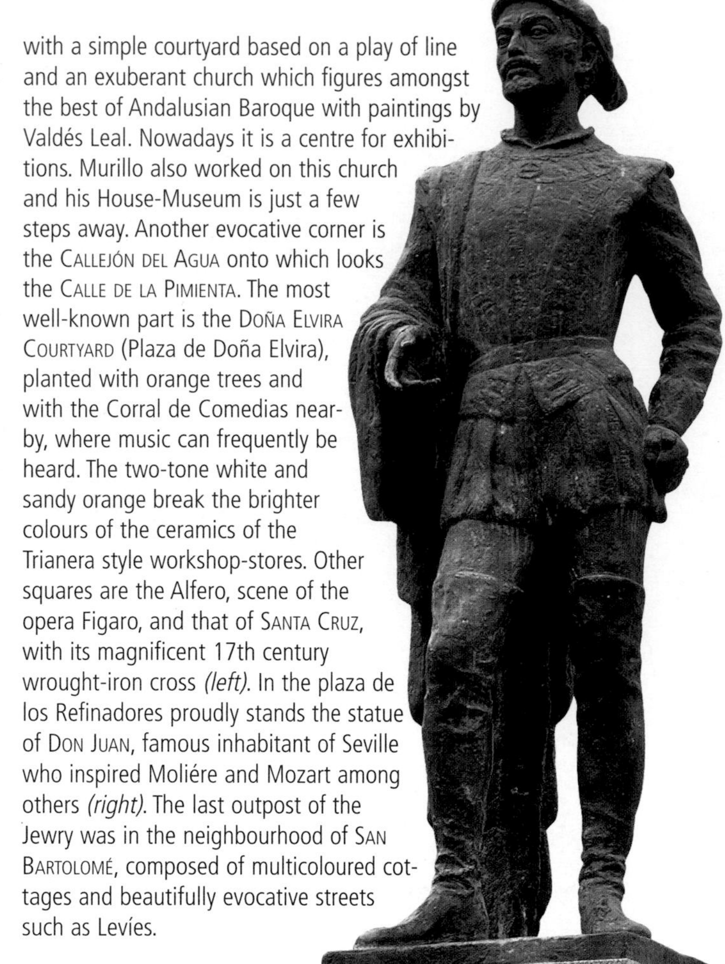

Casa de Pilatos, patio

Above left, one of the large windows of the Casa de Pilatos. Above, Calle de Guzmán el Bueno. On the left, Washington Irving's house at number two, Callejón del Agua.

The Casa de Pilatos

The Renaissance arrived in Spain at the beginning of the 16th century, from cultured noble families like the Tendillas and the Mendozas, who had such a profound influence on 16th century architecture. It was in Seville that Don Fadrique Enríquez, Marquis of Tarifa, dazzled by the splendour of Italian classicism, built this Palace which would serve as a inspiration from 1533 for so many other mansion in the city. Due to its classicist repertoire of the triumphal arch, the façade is reminiscent of Roman villas: in the large courtyard *(previous page, below)* in the centre of which is a double-bodied, Genoese marble fountain dedicated to the god Janus, Gothic balustrades and ceramic work are combined with busts of classical emperors and four sculptures in the corners of Minervas and Ceres. All of this contrasts with the simplicity of the smooth columns which support a stuccoed series of arches displaying a clear Mudéjar influence. The juxtaposition and mixture of such a diverse variety of styles, the wise combination of elements and materials, lends it a sweet balance which represents the synthesis which regionalists called the Sevillian style. Family successors, related to the Medinacelis, completed the outstanding collection of classical works of art and also provided the Palace with gardens, coffered ceilings, etc.

Above left, the tableau of the Entombment by Pedro Roldán on the High Altar of the church in the Hospital de la Caridad which also contains paintings by Murillo and Valdés Leal.

Above right, a detail from the Town Hall, devised with the wedding of Carlos V in mind and created by Diego de Riaño in 1526.

Left, Paso de la Virgin Macarena prepared for the early morning Good Friday procession, the most passionate moment of Holy Week in Seville.

Seville enjoyed the commercial monopoly with America between 1505 and 1717, from where, as well as gold and silver, tobacco, the consumption of which increased at the beginning of the eighteenth century, was imported. The need for large-scale production gave birth to this baroque tobacco factory, a rectangular fortress with a beautiful façade *(right)* and today the seat of the UNIVERSITY. Here, thousands of women worked, among whom one stood out, the gypsy Carmen, the "Cigarrera" by Mérimée.

Although the HOSPITAL DE LA CARIDAD (Charity Hospital) had existed from the fifteenth century it was in 1674 with the building by Don Miguel de Mañara, that the Hermandad de la Caridad became officially recognised. They constructed the Baroque church decorating it with edifying

Above, patio of a stately home. Below, patio in the Hospital de la Caridad

paintings referring to the virtues which the order stood for: mercy and charity. The chosen painters were Valdés Leal who left us two memorable paintings: "In ictu oculti" and "Finis gloriae mundi" dealing with death and the corruption of the body; the second painter, Murillo, produced six masterly canvases which were pillaged by Soult in 1810, although some of the painter's works can still be admired: "San Juan de Dios con un enfermo" and the tenebrist "Santa Isabel de Hungría curando a los tiñosos". The building has two Baroque courtyards designed by Falconete with polygonal fountains in the centre *(right)* with Italian figures again alluding to Mercy and Charity.

Seville also has innumerable churches and convents built between the seventeenth and eighteenth centuries, an era of economic boom, many of them built over old mosques, and the more important monasteries on the outskirts of the city which contributed an iconographic and religious symbolism to Seville, taken to its streets in Holy Week and which in some ways has determined the culture and character of its people.

THE MUSEUMS

From Tartessian times to the present day, such a charismatic city has necessarily had to keep important remains from its past, ranging from the CARAMBOLO TREASURE, wrought in the Bronze Age, to the most recent Baroque in which the schools of Seville held sway. From its days as a Roman capital, we still have Itálica, an open air museum with its Amphitheatre *(above)* and the statue of the Emperor Trajan,

who was born here *(left)*, and an important collection of columns with bas-reliefs, and a collection of mosaics *(right)* some of which line the floors of the capital's mansions.

From the splendid Muslim era which followed, besides the Alcázares and the Giralda there is a magnificent collection of Caliphal capitals.

The FINE ART MUSEUM the second most important collection of paintings in Spain, not surprising considering that the Seville school gave us such geniuses as Velázquez and Murillo.

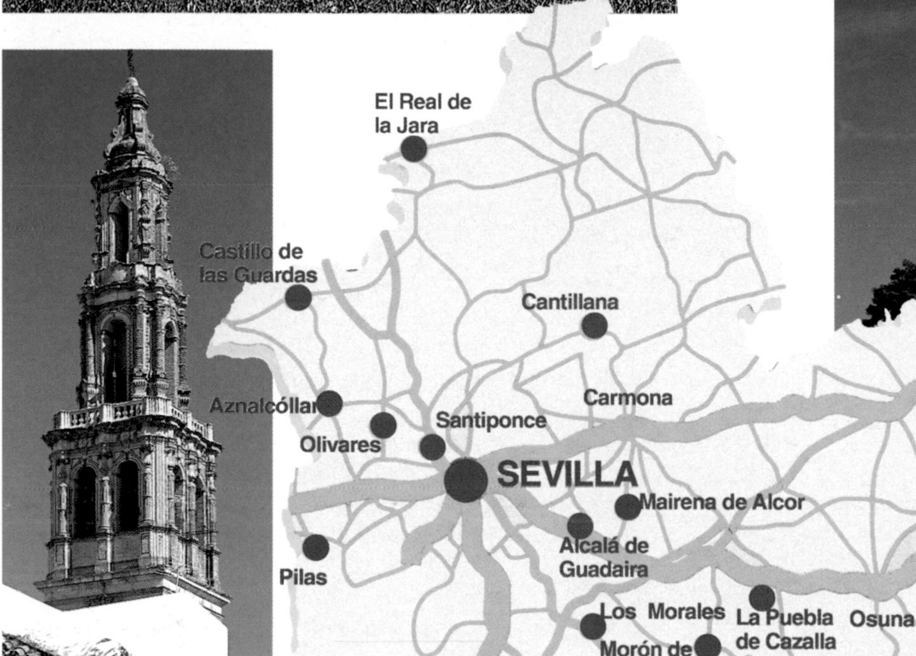

The province of Seville has a mountainous zone which extends into the Sierra Morena, but is mostly developed around the countryside irrigated by the Guadalquivir. Among the many villages, Carmona, Ecija, Osuna, Alcalá stand out, each with its own rich and clearly-defined character.

CORDOBA

The city of Córdoba is scattered along the banks of the Guadalquivir river in whose waters it has been reflected from time immemorial, and set against a backdrop of hills and then mountain ranges (the Sierra Morena) further to the north, and surrounded by the sensual curves of its countryside of infinite wheatfields towards the south until the olive trees appear. Chronicles relate, and remains exist to prove it, that at the beginning of the 11th century, the perimeter of its city wall (22 km) was greater than the space presently occupied by the city in the 21st century. There were other previous Cordobas: there was the "Corduba" of 3,000 years ago on these same banks, which left us the golden pottery, Tartessian settlements had a river port here and the Phoenicians introduced the olive tree, but it was the Romans who turned it into an important colony from 152 B.C. Both Seneca and Lucanus were born here, temples, schools and the bridge which the Augusta road goes over were built, it was the nerve centre of Roman Baética until Seville (Hispalis) took over this position. The best remains of the Visigothic era were saved and incorporated into the mosque. A most splendid past but one shared by other cities until the arrival of the Omayyad Muslims, who nostalgic for and jealous of the Middle East made it theirs and elevated it, on the other side of the Islamic world, to the height of that civilisation and culture. Everyone, including enemies, agreed to recognise caliphal Córdoba as one of the most important cities in the Islamic world, only comparable to Baghdad or Constantinople; such unanimity captures and fuels our imagination since, if our only legacy of the centuries has been ashes of the past, we can only begin to imagine what it must have been like when it was at its most magnificent!

But Cordoba -as Muñoz Molina says, in his book The Córdoba of the Omayyads, which perhaps provides the freshest and most frank look at this city- *"Cordoba is not a decadent city, one of those arrogant cities, suffering from its past, in which life becomes stifling. Córdoba keeps a definitive, underplayed elegance, it is made of the substance of time and the subject of dreams ... there are places in it which seem to contain, hidden and intact, the integrity of the Universe. Córdoba appears to be an allegory, although we realise that we will never be able to reveal the hidden meaning of its beauty or explore in greater detail the silt of successive devastations and wonders erected on ruins which have nourished its survival until now... we are also overwhelmed with the same intensity by Cordoba's splendour and destruction"*. And he adds: *"Cordoba only partially reveals its total beauty to those who wander leisurely around it, to those who discover in each street the secretive wall of a convent or the pillars of the facade of a large deserted palace, or a courtyard with a well which exhales a coolness under the oppression of the heat..."*

Gardens of the Alcázar

Street of the flowers

East façade of the mosque

Crossing of the Cathedral

Roman Bridge

La Calahorra (to

Statue of Maimónides
Roman temple
Typical Patio of Cordoba
Square of the flowers
1. Mezquita Catedral.
2. Palacio de Congresos y Exposiciones.
3. Alcázar de los Reyes Cristianos.
4. Murallas.
5. Triunfo de San Rafael y Puerta del Puente.
6. Puente Romano.
7. Torre de la Calahorra.
8. Molinos Árabes.
9. Calleja de las flores.
10. Sinagoga.
11. Museo Taurino y Zoco.
12. Capilla de San Bartolomé.
13. Casa de las Ceas o del Indiano.
14. Puerta del Almodóvar.
15. Iglesia de la Trinidad.
16. Gobierno militar.
17. Iglesia de San Nicolás de la Villa.
18. Iglesia de San Hipólito.
19. Conservatorio de Música.
20. Iglesia de la Compañía.
21. Iglesia de Santa Victoria.
22. Museo Arqueológico.
23. Arco del Portillo.
24. Casa de los Marqueses del Carpio.
25. Iglesia de San Francisco.
26. Museo Provincial de Bellas Artes y Museo Julio Romero de Torres.
27. Posada del Potro.
28. Plaza de la Corredera.
29. Iglesia de San Pedro.
30. Iglesia de Santiago.
31. Ayuntamiento.
32. Iglesia de San Pablo.
33. Casa de los Villalones.
34. Iglesia de San Andrés.
35. Iglesia de la Magdalena.
36. Círculo de la Amistad.
37. Iglesia de Santa Marta.
38. Plaza de los Dolores.
39. Iglesia de Santa Marina.
40. Palacio de los Marqueses de Viana.
41. Iglesia de San Agustín.
42. Iglesia de San Rafael.
43. Iglesia de San Lorenzo.
44. Convento de los Trinitarios.
45. Iglesia de San Cayetano.
46. Torre de la Malmuerta.
47. Palacio de la Diputación.
Vidal & Vidal
Ediciones Turísticas, S.L.

HISTORY

In the year 711, general Tariq crossed the Strait, which bears his name (Gibraltar), and in only a short time, the Muslims managed to conquer all of the Iberian Peninsula except for some mountainous outposts in the north which were of such little interest that they had not even been Romanised. The key factors behind such a rapid conquest and even of the conversion to Islam can be found in the political crisis of the Visigoths who, with their continual civil wars and taxes, oppressed late Roman society, in the opportunely permissive mood of the Muslims towards the monotheistic believers in the Book (the Bible) and, above all, in the new tax system (2%) which was much less onerous for believers than that of the Visogths. Christian resistance was so sporadic, divided and full of betrayals that it took little more than two years to turn Iberia into the most western province of the Caliphate of Damascus. As well as the new religion, the Arabs brought with them their ancient, tribal customs based on family bonds and clans which gave scant recognition to authorities and hierarchies beyond their circle, and it was this ancient alliance that had formed the basis for the triumph of their religion and the conquest of the world. The Arab leader would always lead his army, he could not retreat and would share out a large part of the booty

among his clients and subjects; he would also comply with the Islamic Jihad which is not carried out against other believers but only against those who oppose the expansion of Islam or attack its beliefs. But in its very success were to be found the seeds of discord from the days of the Prophet: in-fighting between the different families and clans, and the unrest of the North African Berbers who were the most severely affected by the system of land distribution, sparked off the tensions which over time were to favour a political secession of the Abbasid Caliphate and in the long run, the disintegration of the Omayyad Caliphate of al-Andalus in the year 1013.

What happened in Cordoba was not a conquest but rather a capitulation, almost an agreement; five years later, it was made the capital of the emirate which until then had been in Seville. Forty years later, the young Omayyad prince Abderrahman, `the Immigrant´, arrived at the coast of Almuñecar, the sole survivor and fugitive for five years from the fury of the Abbasid Caliph who had brutally massacred his entire family in Damascus (750). With the help of his faithful servant Badr, he had crossed the north of Africa to reach his Berber mother's tribe in Morocco, from where he had also had to flee; but in the end, with the support of the Yemenites, supporters of the Andalusian Omayyads who once again seized

Two views of the Roman Bridge and the Calahorra Tower.
Right the statue of the Archangel Gabriel

the opportunity to rise up, he successfully confronted the Cordoban Emir and proclaimed himself independent of Damascus with the name of Abderrahman I. He always felt a stranger in this land and yearned for the city where he had been born. An expert in the intrigues and betrayals which marked his life, he never integrated into his own court, which was why he built a palace on the outskirts called al-Ruzafa, the same name as the palace where he had grown up in Syria. He is thought to have been responsible for the importation of various species of plants among the many which the Muslims brought to Spain such as pomegranate or palm trees which he planted in the gardens to alleviate his nostalgia for Syria. As any self-respecting Muslim warrior, he also encouraged poetry; he is well known for his lament: "Oh palm tree, like me you are a long way away and a foreigner... like you, I am also a long way away from my home, may the clouds of the soul grant you coolness in this remoteness and the abundant rain always console you" or "for me, more pleasing than sublime gardens or palaces are the desert and living in tents".

He surrounded himself with a mercenary army since he no longer trusted his own people but he laid the foundations of a strong, organised power on such a disperse and difficult to govern territory. And he ruled as an absolute sovereign, in the Omayyad style, without delegating power to the officials who served him and not accounting to anyone.This smoothed the way, for his successors, not without surprises and revolts, but which would bring about the appearance of the independent caliphate. He lived for many years and with enough time to make improvements to palaces, to rebuild walls including the city wall of Cordoba, to erect mosques which have been accurately dated, and above all, to begin the Friday mosque, the most important construction in an Islamic city, Córdoba's great Mezquita-Aljaima, the most outstanding construction of universal Spanish-Muslim work. The increase in the number of believers meant that there was no longer enough space in the St. Vincent church which the Muslims shared with the Christians having bought half of it from the Visigoths after the conquest for their Friday prayers. Between the years 784-786 they bought the other half of the basilica, compensating the Christians very well financially and allowing them to build new churches in other parts of the city. Work on the new mosque was carried out in a record time thanks to the use of materials which already existed in the basilica and a large quantity of building elements such as bases, capitals, shafts and pillars brought from nearby Roman and Visigothic palaces and ruins. The leaders played an important role in the building work which they had commissioned; specialists wonder whether Abderrahman himself was the architect for his mosque or if he had ordered Syrian architects to be brought over, but it is not known to what extent he took part in the building work; there is, however, a clear Syrian influence, and it was this, together with superior local genius and the creativity and contribution of new architectural decorative features, which would make the Cordoban mosque a model to follow and whose influence would then spread back to the regions from where it had originated.

On the death of Abderrahman (788) work had not been finished although it had been possible to pray there in the year after work had begun (785) but the mosque was not declared finished until his son Hishan II completed it in the year 793, having built the square-plan minaret in the northern part of the Patio de Abluciones o de los Naranjos (Courtyard of Ablutions or of the Orange trees).

The Mezquita of Córdoba is one of the most outstanding architectural constructions in the world, the most important example of Islamic art in the west and one of the most significant works in absolute terms, both for its technical and aesthetic innovations and its influence on art history. Having survived for more than twelve centuries, it continues to command admiration at the beginning of the third millennium and, as would be expected, throughout such an extensive existence has had to overcome respectful additions during its first three centuries and has suffered radical alterations over the last five, for which we should be grateful that it has survived at all. On the other hand, together with the ruins of Medina Zahara, it is almost the only testimony left us by a culture which dazzled its contemporaries and which has survived for so long in a strange world for the mere fact of being a holy space. Fortunately, and in spite of everything, the ethereal space miraculously trapped inside remains almost intact, framed by the fragile forms of its arches where thousands of perfectly lined up faithful would congregate for Friday prayers. In this computer age, it is tempting to make a hypothetical reconstruction of its original forms and sizes *(on the right)* but although this can give us some idea, it is no substitute for the necessary imagination.

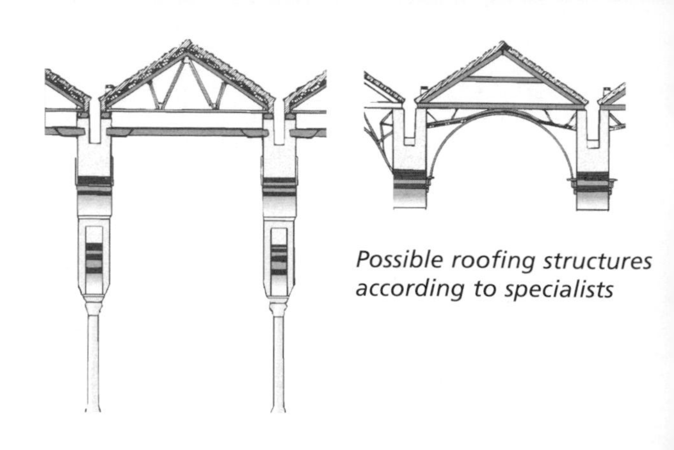

Possible roofing structures according to specialists

The last eight eastern naves were added at the end of the first millennium by Almanzor in an attempt to please the religious leaders and as a result of yet another considerable population increase. It was the most uniform and least innovative extension.

The covered portico which surrounds the courtyard was added by Abderrahman III. Previously, there had only been a 3.5m high wall.

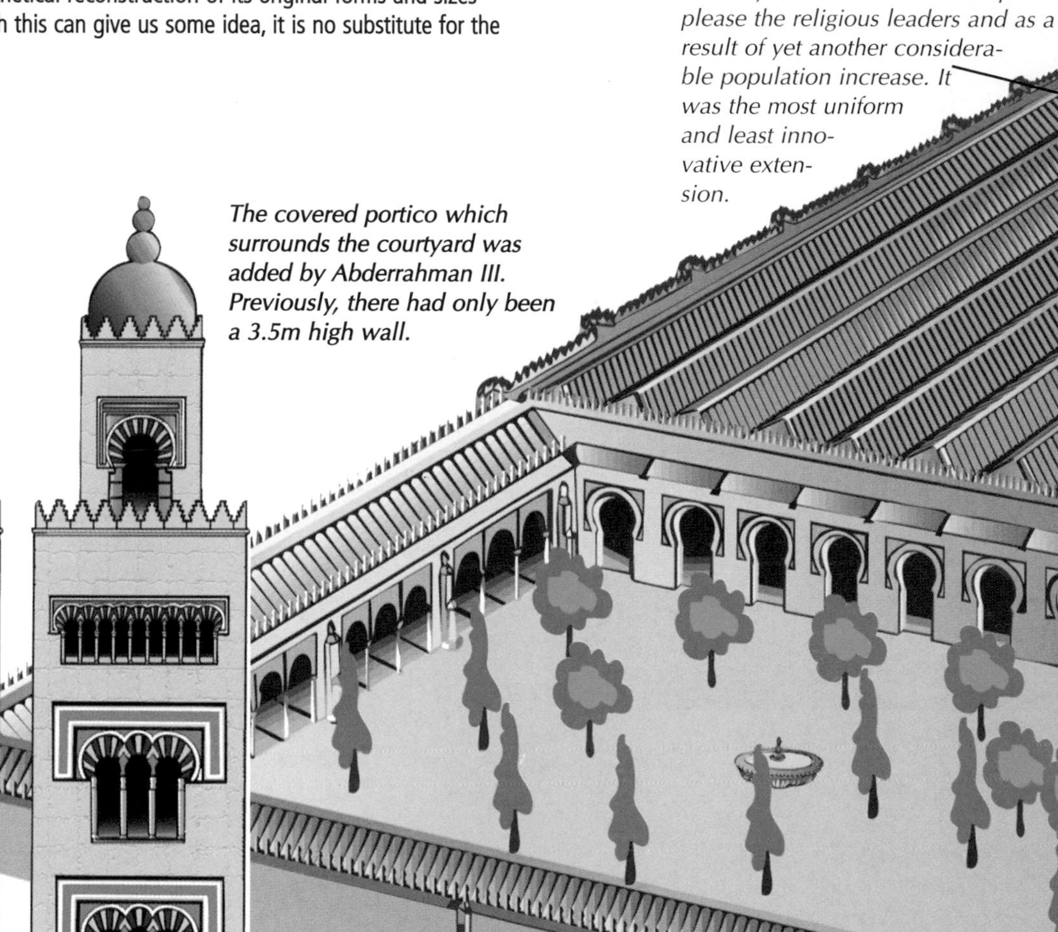

North-South side ***East-West side***

Minaret means "the place of light": the place from where the Word is spread which enlightens the soul as of light clears the shade (M. Molina). There has been much speculation about the second minaret, the one built by Abderrahman III. For some it was topped with three balls, for others with five. It was 47.5 m. high. As with the Giralda, Hernán Ruiz II added a double section for the bells and the clock in 1593 but subsequently, and because of earthquakes, an outer layer was built which hid what remained of it. Don Félix Hernández, who studied it in depth, left us the drawings which have been used as a model for these computer graphic reconstructions (left). One thing that is certain is that its form and structure survived in all subsequent constructions including those of Marrakech, Rabat and the Giralda as well as some contemporary ones such as church towers today in Andalusia and of course, in Romanesque art even on the other side of the Pyrenees.

Puerta del Perdón, S.

Modifications made to the Mezquita over the years.

1. **Construction by Abderrahman I. Year 785**
2. **Extension by Abderrahman II. Year 833**
3. **Addition by Abderrahman III. Year 945**
4. **The Maqsura and the Mihrab . Al-Hakam II. Year 961**
5. **The Extension of Almanzor. Year 987.**
6. **The Courtyard of the Orange Trees (Patio de los Naranjos).**
7. **The minaret.**

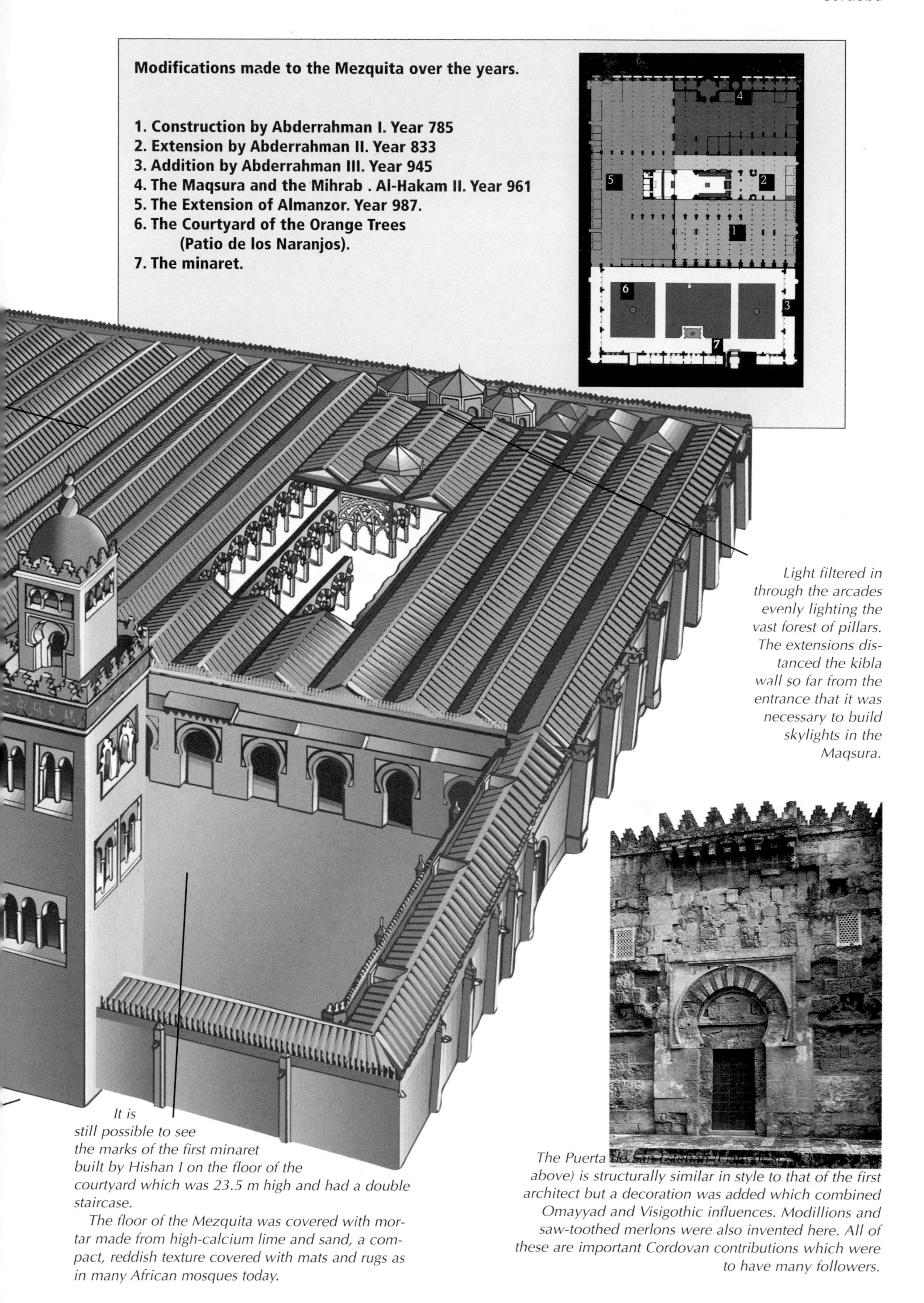

Light filtered in through the arcades evenly lighting the vast forest of pillars. The extensions distanced the kibla wall so far from the entrance that it was necessary to build skylights in the Maqsura.

It is still possible to see the marks of the first minaret built by Hishan I on the floor of the courtyard which was 23.5 m high and had a double staircase.

The floor of the Mezquita was covered with mortar made from high-calcium lime and sand, a compact, reddish texture covered with mats and rugs as in many African mosques today.

The Puerta de San Esteban (Gate of St. [illegible] above) is structurally similar in style to that of the first architect but a decoration was added which combined Omayyad and Visigothic influences. Modillions and saw-toothed merlons were also invented here. All of these are important Cordovan contributions which were to have many followers.

The Mosque

The Mezquita, a word which means a place to prostrate oneself, had originated in the Prophet's house where he would meet with believers for the Friday prayers. It was an open courtyard with palm tree trunks supporting brushwood which offered protection from the sun. At first, there was nothing more than the walls of the courtyard and those of his own house, there was not even a clear direction until Mohammed placed a stick on the wall to direct prayer towards Jerusalem, a direction which was then changed for that of Mecca. At first, mosques lacked a well-defined spatiality; it was contact with the conquered villages of Greco-Roman, Persian and, in particular, Byzantine tradition that provided the first caliphs with the elements and patterns which needed to be quickly assimilated and which would give rise to Islamic art, which was perfected in only a short period of time. There was no architectural tradition in the desert, at the most a preference for wide areas determined by the horizontality of space, by the open air and, with the appearance of Islam, the need to determine a point on the horizon. That is why the basilical model which was widely used in the conquered territories would quickly be adopted to build mosques with parallel naves, almost omnidirectional, with no axial direction but aligned for prayer and indicating the direction of Mecca by means of the kibla or orientative wall in which the *mihrab* would be placed. It was only at a later stage that the *mihrab* would come to be regarded as a holy place.

On the left, the Façade of the Gate of Al Hakam II , with crossed latticework above of Visigothic origin and on the right, the gate of Almanzor's extension restored at the beginning of the 20th century.

The first Mezquitas after that of the Medina, were those at Kufa (638) and Amrú (642) which already had pillars made with bricks; shortly afterwards, the Omayyads, the true pioneers of Islamic architecture, erected the Dome of the Rock in Jerusalem (687). But the mosques which started the architectural tradition in the first few years of the 8th century, and whose influence guided the incipient Islamic art, were those of Damascus in Syria (707) and that of al-Aksa in Jerusalem. All of them greatly marked by pre-Islamic basilical heritage, with naves parallel to the *kibla* comprising arches, some pointed, which support a continuous thick wall like an impost on which a second floor can be built with a smaller arcade to lighten the load and let the light through. The Syrian influence spread throughout North Africa to Cordoba where, 80 years later, it would receive an innovative impetus which would in many cases outclass the models.

The Exterior of the Mezquita

Including the courtyard, the Mezquita today has a surface area of 23,118 m2 forming a large rectangle of almost 130x180m although its original size (76x75m) only had 11 naves with 12 files of columns, as you can see in the approximate reconstruction which appears opposite. In the course of three centuries, extensions and alterations were made by the three Abderrahmans: I, II and III, and their reigns were marked by successive extensions and the moments of greatest Cordoban splendour within each century (8th,9th and 10th) culminating with the son of the last Abderrahman, al-Hakam II, who, in 961 completed his father's work, contributing the most spectacular innovations in the mihrab which we know today and the cupolas which precede it in the maqsura. The later extension by general Almanzor was nothing more than a secondary addition, as was the alteration of the structure of the Cathedral Church.

Above and Right: Two views of the Riwat or Columned Arcade of the Sahn (patio)

Originally, the sahn or the Courtyard of the Ablutions (Patio de las Abluciones) *(above)* was only closed by a simple wall which in the time of Abderrahman III (10th cent.) was reinforced and completed by the arcades under which the greatest part of daily activity would take place. As well as being a place to worship, the Mezquita, with its courtyard,

the equivalent of a public square in the West, where people meet to talk or just be; there was even a mint in these porticos with its resulting hustle and bustle. A fundamental element in all mosques is the fountain which is used for the obligatory ritual purifications. At first, water was drawn here from an artesian well but from 961 onwards, the necessary water was supplied from the Sierra and was then stored in the large cistern built by Almanzor. The five Baroque fountains now in the courtyard date from the 17th and 18th centuries.

As in other mosques, the arches giving entry to the prayer area were not closed, so that *"light could shine through unhindered and pass through the open walls and lattices because it was the symbol of divine light, which penetrates the most hidden places, intelligence and men's hearts. The lattice is a wall which becomes transparent and surrenders to the light: the mosque opens itself to the light, and its architecture seems not to be constructed with solid materials but rather with modulations of light and shade..."* (Muñoz Molina).

Today there are twelve gates, of which the five western ones, the oldest, give us information about different extensions and the architectural evolution of each period. The innovations which stand out the most on the outside wall are the various scrolled modillions and the Cordoban saw-toothed merlons. The Gate or postern of St. Stephen built in 855-856, became the model for subsequent gates after the first extension was finished. Its decoration is a synthesis of the style of the Visigoths and that of the Caliphate. Here new forms were created, combining influences from the Middle East and the use of indigenous materials and techniques, providing a new and successful fusion, such as the blind horse-shoe arch decoratively inscribed in Arabic. This arch consists of alternating voussoirs made of red brick and stucco work (instead of stone). In this way they repeated on the external facade the same figures that had been invented one hundred years earlier and used in the interior, but this time using a more elaborate organic design of Omayyad origin.

Hypothetical recreation of the first Mosque (785).

Once again, forms which had originally been solely decorative or accidentally gained a constructive value while at the same time those which had been previously of an essentially constructive nature were transformed into decorative shapes.

This pleasing combination, which demonstrates a genius for synthesis on its creator's part, was also turned into the model for the *mihrab*, the blind arches of Medina Zahara and numerous others which followed these Cordoban guidelines, including Mozarabic and Romanesque art.

The Interior of the Mezquita

Even if familiar with other Mosques, on entering The Alijaima in Cordoba you have the sensation of being transferred to a very different and sacred place, a space which expands in every direction, in which transparent arches hang like weightless palm trees. Hardly supported, they form an enormous spider' s web seeking the transcendental.

"The pillars affirm their verticality over the capitals like branches which rise up higher and higher searching for light. The red and white voussoirs emphasise the sensation of a space repeated and expanded towards the unreachable limit of the distant horizon". (A. Muñez Molina). The perfect parallelism between the floor and the ceiling converges for the Muslim believers in an infinite proportion, a mystical nothingness, a place of revelation in their personal encounter with God.

The solution to the problem of how to construct the main building led to a decisive breakthrough in world architecture. The first problem was that the Roman and Visigothic columns which were being re-used here were of different heights and on average shorter than was customary in Syrian architecture, the model for mosques. This was resolved by deciding on a fixed height-line from which the tops of the columns would 'hang' and when they were too short, bases of different heights were added and when too long they were set into the ground.

The two-tone effect produced by the combination of red brick and limestone arranged radially was so successful that it was widley used in Muslim and Romanesque architecture.

The fact that the height-line was still too low to put the roof on meant that a solution had to be found to extend the columns upwards. This was done by placing massive rectangular piers on top of them with tiers of arches between, the lower horse-shoe arches and the upper rounded. This may have been inspired by the Roman aqueduct at Mérida. Since these piers were far wider than the columns they had to be bevelled-off at the lower end with modillions, these were then carved with scroll decoration. An abacus was invented to seat the piers on top of the columns just over the capitals and complete the transition from slender column to heavy

pier. The abacus is a stone block rather like an upside-down truncated pyramid. This brilliant solution in which the horse-shoe arches springing from this abacus act as a buttress for the enormous weight above but do not block-up the upper space is proof of the great genius of the unknown architect.

Stierlin states *"never before had internal spaces so vast been conceived, made with a method as simple as that of columns supporting arches of limited dimensions. Neither the hypostyle chambers of the Pharaonic temples (Karnak, Luxor), nor the Roman basilicas nor the Constantine churches bore any comparison. Never had spaces been so light or so transparent. Probably only the great Roman and Byzantine cisterns had given birth to such schemes as this"*.

Without ignoring the influence of the mosque at Damascus, another noticeable improvement in the mosque at Cordoba, is that the naves are perpendicular, not parallel to the *Kibla*, the centre-point which leads to the widest *mihrab* in the style of a basilica. The naves mark a converging direction towards this point, without breaking the uniformity of the space. Don Enrique Pareja says that in principle, the horse-shoe arch and the simple leaf capital had been inherited from the Hispano-Visigothic world, and the figurative representation from the Byzantine. The genuinely Omayyad elements would be the transept, the square-plan minarets, the mosaics and the domes; from their Abbasid enemies they adopted the lobed arches and the stylisation of the forms. The ribbed vaults, the inlaid decoration, and the deeply carved marble capitals would be of Cordoban creation.

Although the mosque was built over the course of more than two hundred years with continual additions, these respected the original work, perhaps in part in recognition of its creators, but above all because it contained all the elements and technical and aesthetic discoveries of a masterpiece. Hishan I (788-796) completed the work of his father Abderrahman I, building the first minaret. Forty years later the second Abderrahman (822-852) undertook the first extension of the chamber (833) adding eight new sections, half the area of which has now been lost within the Cathedral. The extension which took fifteen years was directed by Masrur and Nasr who also used old columns but without bases, and eleven capitals of roman influence purposefully created for the Mezquita. In the era of Abderrahman II, the emirate reached a previously unknown splendour; a powerful Middle Eastern influence which arrived from Baghdad under the leadership of Ziryab.

The lobed arches of the Abbasid tradition (above and below) lend it a lightness; even while being its strongest element they are criss-crossed like a spider's web, creating unravelling lines to beautiful effect.

The Caliphal Mosque

Above, the Almanzor extension which, near the end of the millennium, demonstrated no new architectural advances. Right, the arch of the Mihrab, greatest example of Caliphal art.

The reign of Abderrahman III, which lasted more than fifty years, began in the middle of the revolts and wars inherited from his grandfather (912) which he was able to put an end to after twenty years of fighting with Omar Ibn Hafsun, the Christians from the north and the African Fatimids in order to proclaim himself Caliph in the year 929, thus affirming his independence and power. Among the many works that he had built, such as his palace in Medina Zahara (936), was the new Mezquita minaret (951) forty-eight metres in height, of which only twenty-two metres remain encased in the modern tower. This minaret then influenced all Western Islamic minarets. Enlarging the patio necessarily entailed making alterations, such as extending it an additional sixty metres to the north and surrounding it on three sides with the Riwat, the colonnaded gallery six metres deep with alternating pillars and columns.

But it was his son al-Hakam II, the devout and well-educated prince who had ruled over Medina Zahara for years, who, the day after succeeding the throne, undertook the extension of the Mezquita which was once again too small for the increase in the population. Demolishing the *kibla* wall, he moved twelve sections as far south as the river allowed in such a way that the length of the prayer area reached almost 104 metres. He also raised the *Maqsura* so that for the second time in the history of the Mezquita brilliant and original breakthroughs were made, a completely new structural system destined to make history in the architectural world. In doing so, he achieved a harmonious distribution in accordance with the first master from the eighth century. All this new space was overlooked by a facade with multi-lobed arches which preceded the *Mihrab* (right), the true focal point.

The Maqsura and the Mihrab

For the extension of Al-Hakam II (961), the most important so far, materials were not transported from elsewhere. Instead, columns and capitals came from the Caliph's workshops. Lack of light and ventilation made it necessary to construct the four skylights and once again necessity gave rise to an ingenious solution. The necessary supports, more solid than the previous ones, seem to multiply their lightness because of the depth resulting from the crossing of the lobed domes, but the links are ribs which cross each other creating sections within the central intersection. This creates contrasting tensions and increases the redistribution of weight as well as achieving a beautiful effect. From this framework the ribbed cupola *(above)*, which almost seems to float, rises up. Its design has an octagonal format, six metres in diameter, with eight finely veined arches forming two intertwined squares placed at a forty-five degree angle to support them. These cross-ribs act as an arch, dividing the space into small segments and now so much easier to vault as the vault itself is made of stone and not of brick like the Persian ones, a century later.

THE MIHRAB appeared in Medina with the Omayyad reconstruction of its mosque, but it was in Cordoba that it reached its most refined expression and for the first time it was turned into a recess within the *Kibla*. Perhaps under the influence of the Christian apse or the Roman recesses for their divine statues. What had previously been a small cleft was transformed into a niche with eight sides, capped with a semispherical dome in the shape of a shell and a symbol of life and of the divine word.

On special occasions a book of the Qur'an, hand-written by the Oman, was placed below this dome. It was converted into a setting for prostration before Allah, a symbolic gate which leads to a beyond towards which prayers ascend; a symbol of the absolute, an affirmation of the divine within this world. What had begun as a simple point of reference, here came to fruition as the meeting point of transcendent religious meaning. Any place may be sacred and suitable for prayer:

"Whichever way you turn, there is the face of God. But the *mihrab* must be the most suitable place because it magnetises the eyes in order to direct them towards distant Mecca". On the other hand its orientation isn't entirely correct, and although there has been much discussion over the reasons for the deviation (17° further south) there is no real explanation. Accordingly, for some authors it followed the orientation of St. Vicent, whereas for others it copied the orientation of the mosque at Damascus, from where its founder came. Whatever the case may be, we are dealing with a masterpiece in which al-Hakam II, who many years earlier had overseen the works of Medina Zahara, managed to express the splendour and maturity of Caliphal art with its clear oriental influence. In order to do so he didn't hesitate in asking the Christian Emperor Consantinopla Niceforo Focas for help, just as the first Omayyad in Damascus had done 250 years earlier. While Charlemagne was forming an alliance with the Abbasids, the Cordovan Omayyads did the same with The Eastern Christian Empire. For this collaboration he received not only pieces of brightly coloured glass weighing 32,000 pounds, some of which were laminated in gold, but also the master craftsman who taught the Cordobans the Byzantine mosaic technique.

As Gómez Moreno says, it is necessary to go back to St. Sophia in order to find anything comparable in fineness and elegance. Muñoz Molina adds: "*The light of the lamps would blindingly pierce the surface of the marble, the glass and the gold of the mosaics, moist with the perfumes sprinkled over them. The light and the geometry of the arabesques broke up the impenetrability of the wall*". "*The arabesque allows the void to enter the heart of the material, to undo its opacity and to make it transparent to the light of God*" (Hussain Nasr).

Above left, ribbed cupola and below, multicoloured wooden roof.

Right, Roman alabaster column and below, view of the Maqsura and the Mihrab.

The first Mezquita has almost 150 capitals brought from other Visigothic and Roman monuments, transported material which represents a large collection of styles from the first seven centuries of our era. Their worth therefore varies greatly, from the highly elaborate Corinthian capitals of the Classical and late Roman era, to those of the Visigoths with a sometimes simple and unrefined touch, yet full of ingenious elegance: these are the well-known simple leaf capitals. They are often decorated, and the four corners finished off with stylised Ionic scrolls. For the first extension (9th cent.) although pre-Islamic capitals were also used, eleven new ones were produced by the Cordovan workshops who for reasons of uniformity copied the previous ones. The abaci, the stone blocks just above the capitals are once again of Christian-Visigothic origin (seventeen in total for this extension) with geometric decoration and vine-leaves including Christian crosses. The Caliphal capital (10th cent.), derived from the Roman Corinth capital, and much used in Medina Zahara, had insinuated or outlined alcanthine leaves carved on each base with their multiplying leaves becoming finer. The resulting effect was to become known as the "wasp's nest capital" and would continue to be developed until the 15th Nazari century.

Above, six examples of the collection of capitals used in the Cordoban Mezquita, the ideal place, according to Gómez Moreno, to study the evolution of the classic capital and its transformation into Visigothic art, and as if in a museum, they probably would not have survived if the arquitect had not had the happy idea to re-use them here.

Right, multi-lobed arches of the Villaviciosa chapel which precede the maqsura marking a space in front of the mihrab destined for the Caliph, defined by th width of its three naves, including the central one. This design which seems to copy the ico nostasis of Christian churches is against the sp rit of Islam in which there is no difference whatsoever between the faithful. It is the last stage in the development of Caliphal art whic is completely unlike the aesthetic sensitivity c the original construction. This model of inter crossed, multi-lobed arches, later so imitated, creates a closure effect which helps to highlight the consecrated area of the Mezquita.

The Christianisation of the Mezquita after the conquest of the city (1236) did not entail any substantial alterations to the building, but in 1523 Bishop Alonso Manrique, the uncle of the Emperor Charles V, managed to obtain his nephew's permission for the construction of the Gothic nave in its interior. The Emperor would regret this later upon seeing it during his wedding trip. But work continued for almost a century under Hernán Ruiz I, Hernán Ruiz II and Juan de Ochoa. It was only in 1766 that it was totally completed and since it was only natural that tastes should change over the years, it was Hernán Ruiz himself who suggested the transition to the Renaissance, moving through Plateresque, to the richest Baroque and finally the Churrigueresque. The High Altar is an example of this mixture: the arches of the Latin cross are Gothic, whereas the vaults of the central nave and the Crossing are in Herrera's style *(above)*

THE CATHEDRAL

The altarpiece (1618) is by the Jesuit master Alonso Matías made in red marble and Cordoban jasper from Carcabuey and Cabra which act as frames for the paintings by Palomino. The two pulpits by Verdiguier are worthy of note, carved in mahogany and supported by the symbols of the four evangelists, each carved in different coloured stone (below left the Lion of St. Mark in red veined marble). But standing out above all are the choir stalls, made of Cuban mahogany by Pedro Duque Cornejo in the middle of the 18th Century, which touch in a masterly fashion on a varied anthology of religious themes from the biblical to Cordovan martyrology.

Between the uniformity of stalls the episco-

Previous page above, the Crossing. *Above, the choir stalls in Cuban mahogany by Duque Cornejo*

pal throne stands out *(above)* in which Baroque rhetoric displays all its capacity for meaning: the Lord's Ascension witnessed by the apostles, crowned by the archangel St. Raphael, patron saint of the city and framed by St. Theresa and Mary Magdalene, whose exemplary lives acquired great doctrinal prominence.

The Cathedral also has more than fifty chapels many of them against the walls, among which the chapel of Cardinal Salazar, also called the Chapel of St. Theresa, stands out since there is a magnificent sculpture of the Saint by José de Mora above it. As well as the Sacristy, it is also the Chapterhouse with its typical octagonal Baroque design, decorated by Hurtado Izquierdo, another of the last great Baroque masters together with Duque Cornejo and Palomino, who did the paintings. Next to it is the treasury containing Enrique Arfe´s famous monstrance, in Gothic style although dating from the 16th. century. It measures 2.63m and weighs more than 200kg. Among the many precious objects of worship there is a crucifix by Alonso Cano and another of the thirteenth century.

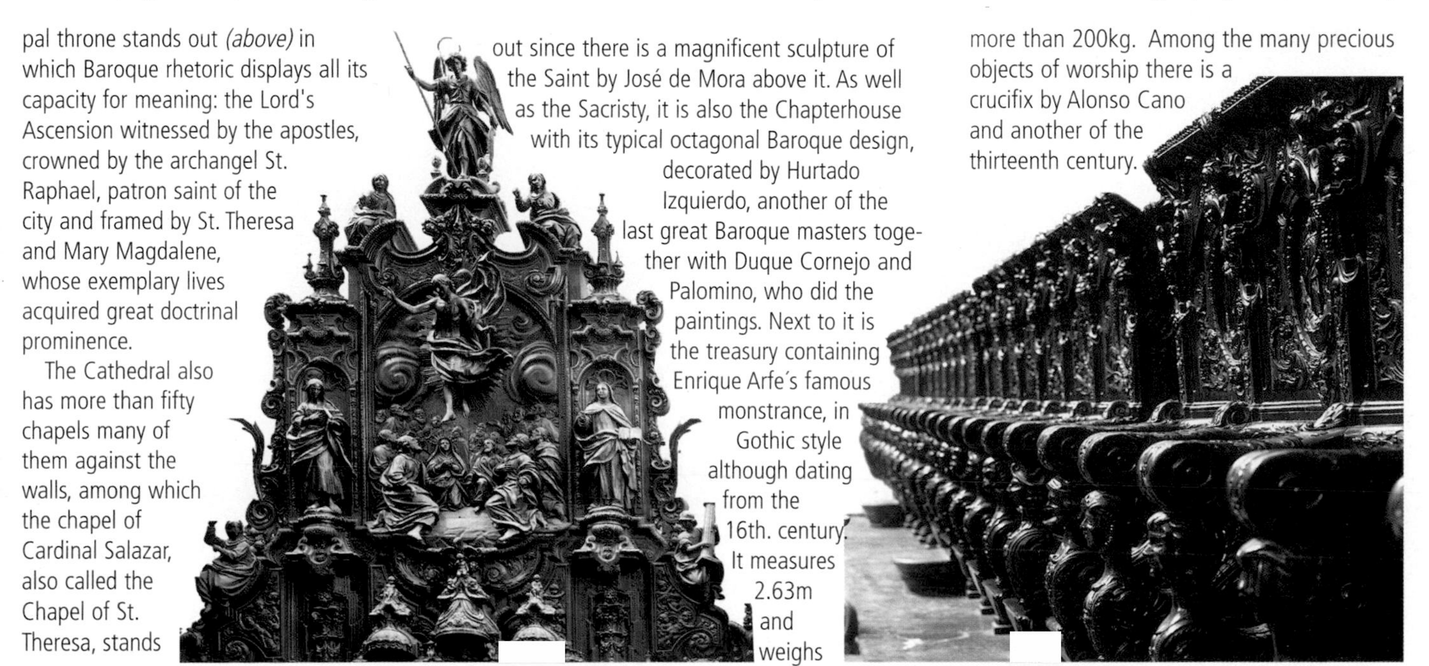

5

THE ALCÁZAR

In the area around the Mezquita and on Roman and Arabic remains, Alfonso XI ordered the Alcázar of the Catholic Monarchs to be built, so-named to distinguish it from the one used by the emirs nearby. It is a square fortress with towers at the corners, joined by a long gallery lined with valuable archaeological pieces such as the remarkable Roman Sarcophagus (3rd C.), and the great hall of mosaics, some, like the ones by Poliferno and Galatea (2nd C.), with the most beautiful colours. It was the scene of the first meetings with Columbus (1486), the prison of the Inquisition, and a civil and military prison until 1951. The appearance of the gardens with their five pools has changed.

The synagogue is another of the treasures of Cordoba lost in the complex maze of streets and courtyards of the Jewish quarter (la Judería). It was also constructed under the tolerant reign of Alfonso XI (1315) in the Mudéjar style, decorated with plasterwork and inscriptions in Hebrew. This community was the seat of the greatest Jewish theologian of all time, Ben Maimonedes (1112-1185) who compiled the Torah, summarising its principles in thirteen. To him we owe the Spanish saying, "mantenerse en sus trece (thirteen)" or "to stand one's ground". His statue *(left)* can be found beside the Synagogue. Cordovan thinkers are as significant as their monuments: the figure of the philosopher AVERROES *(above)* watches over one of the gates of the city wall as do those of SENECA and IBN-HAZAM at another. From the early Christian conquest (1236) numerous churches have been erected, ranging from the Gothic to the Baroque, such as those of St. Paul, St. Andrew, St. Lawrence, St. Francis, St. Raphael, etc. In order to take a closer look at Cordoba's history, a visit to the Archaeological Museum, the most important in the city and the second in Spain, is essential, although there are other museums such as the one in the Plaza del Potro (of the colt), or the Museum of Fine Art, the Julio Romero de Torres Museum and the Museum of Bullfighting in the Jewish quarter. The Viana Palace-Museum, a national monument, possesses a collection of art as important as the building itself with its twelve courtyards.

On the left, Cordovan patios decorated for the Festival of the Cross (3rd May). Below the Colt Inn (Posada del Potro).

MEDINA ZAHARA

Like the Abbasid Caliphs in Bagdad, Abderrahman III chose to build his palatine city on the outskirts of the town and he settled on Mount al-Arus near Cordoba. It took forty years to build yet only survived thirty-four. Chronicles report that there were ten thousand men working on the construction, with six thousand blocks being carved each day and more than four thousand columns brought from all corners of the Caliphate. Although these figures were previously thought to be exaggerated, they seem to be confirmed by research, and al-Hakam II appears to have directed the work in which Caliphal Art absorbed and combined Eastern Syrian motifs and Byzantine influences in order to create new forms and original repertoires more exquisite than their age suggests.
The city extends 1,518m from East to West, and 745m from North to South, stretching across three large terraces with irregular and uneven terrain (70m). The upper terrace was for the Caliph's residence from where he controlled the entire complex and ruled his court. The middle terrace was taken up with administration, gardens, court rooms and the living quarters of the higher officials. The lower terrace, where the Mezquita, baths, houses, souks were also to be found, was the area where the common people and the troops lived.
In the middle of the upper BRILLIANT TERRACE was the main chamber, surrounded on the east side by three rooms used as the official reception area, and the octagonal Throne-room with its eight doors behind "...the marble and ebony arches, the varied transparent jasper and marble walls, the golden mosaic domed ceilings, covered in gold and silver tiles...". In the middle of the city is the large square with sides of 100m, walled by the central terrace to the north with a pool which leads to the Rich Chamber *(Salón Rico, below)*. This chamber which is also known as the Pavilion of Abderrahman III has a rectangular floor and five naves, the central three of which are above a series of arches *(right)* and the other two behind the walls. What particularly stands out in this chamber is the more refined Caliphal style of decoration, with the ornamentation of the bases, the two-tone effect of the alternate red and green columns, and the sophisticated deeply carved capitals. The marble slabs which cover the walls have a soft appearance, with simple relief, and long stems and

On the left and on the previous page above, the Casa de los Visires (House of the Viziers) also known as the Casa del Ejército (Army House) situated to the north, next to the five-metre-thick wall which protected the city and close to the lowest series of porticoed arches. Only a very small part of what lies buried in the archaeological site has come to light in the excavations, nearly all of which were carried out in the twentieth century, as previously their location had been unknown. Fortunately previous treasure-hunters had underestimated the value of the artefacts.

realistic leaves. As Professor Pareja says, *"in the hands of skilled craftsmen, marble becomes a yielding material ... the plant decoration invades the plinths as if wishing to create a hedge from which the walls emerge"*. And he adds, *"A completely new and different process was started in Medina Zahara which would prove the quality of the workshops which were to forge the new Cordovan Caliphal art ... an art which managed to escape monotony and routine."*

On the right, a marble flagstone with an image representing the tree of life from Syria. It consists of a central trunk which branches out and twists, with broadly symbolic leaves and flowers until it fills the whole panel. New oriental influences from the "Second Style" can be seen in the carving and the base, which Professor D. Enrique Pareja López considers to be more realistic.

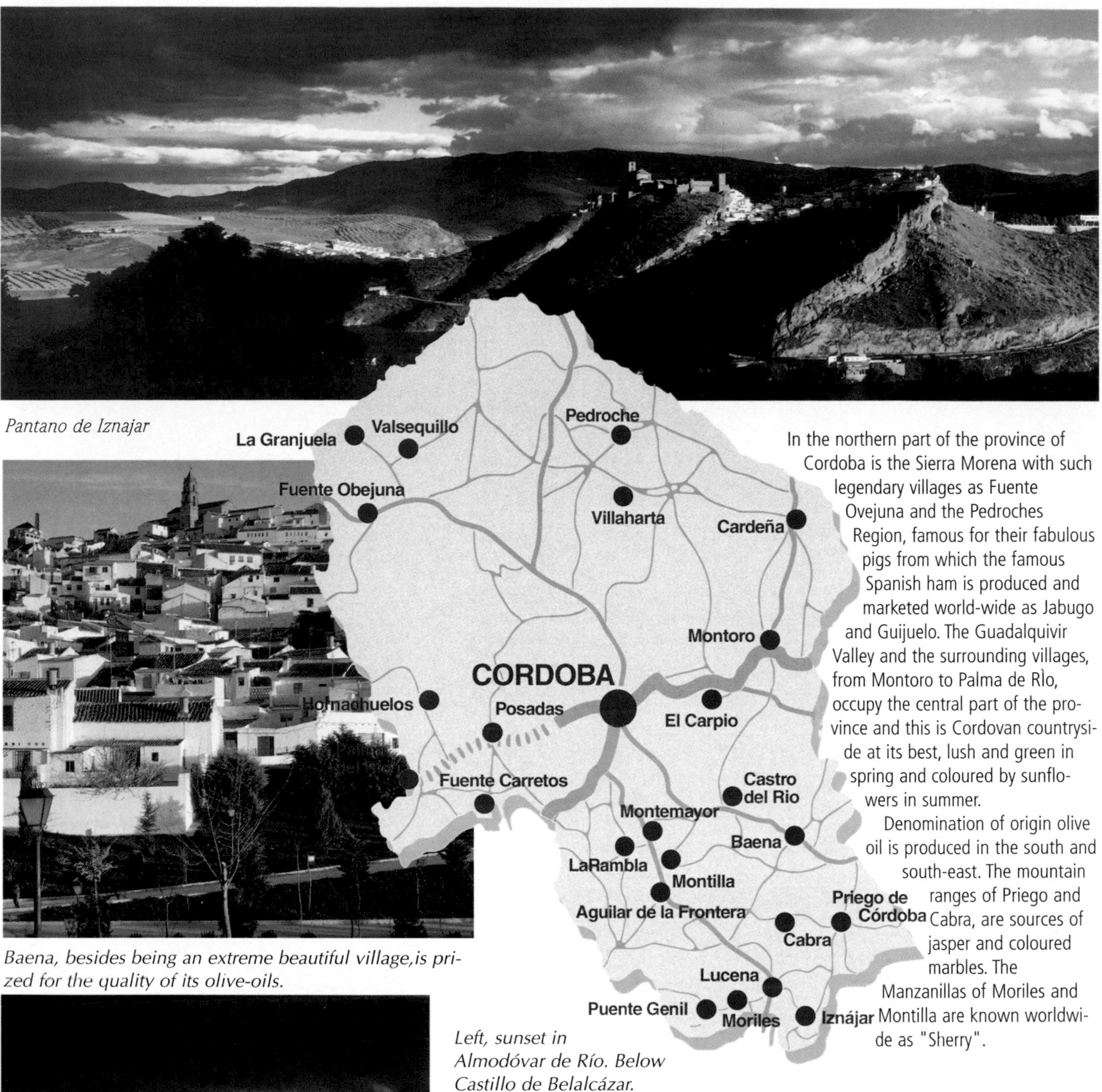

Pantano de Iznajar

Baena, besides being an extreme beautiful village,is prized for the quality of its olive-oils.

In the northern part of the province of Cordoba is the Sierra Morena with such legendary villages as Fuente Ovejuna and the Pedroches Region, famous for their fabulous pigs from which the famous Spanish ham is produced and marketed world-wide as Jabugo and Guijuelo. The Guadalquivir Valley and the surrounding villages, from Montoro to Palma de Rìo, occupy the central part of the province and this is Cordovan countryside at its best, lush and green in spring and coloured by sunflowers in summer.

Denomination of origin olive oil is produced in the south and south-east. The mountain ranges of Priego and Cabra, are sources of jasper and coloured marbles. The Manzanillas of Moriles and Montilla are known worldwide as "Sherry".

Left, sunset in Almodóvar de Río. Below Castillo de Belalcázar.

JAEN

Sandwiched between Castile and Andalusia, the province of Jaén has a share in both without losing its particular personality. Half tableland, half mountainous terrain, it is bordered by the Sierra Morena and the Sierra del Cambrón in the north, the Sierra del Segura in the east, the Southern Sierras in the south, and Cordoba and Lower Andalusia in the west. The Guadalquivir, which rises in its mountain ranges, drains the entire province, while olive trees adorn almost half of its terrain. Its landscapes are unmistakable: armies of perfectly-lined, silver-green olive trees standing on brownish-grey hills speak of a region that

is almost entirely given over to agriculture. The typically Mediterranean olive tree has dominated these lands since the 19th century when intensive and extensive estate farming was introduced. More and better quality olive oil is produced here than in any other region in Spain. Now, in the 21st century, when its culinary and medicinal qualities have finally been recognised, it is destined to play an important part in healthy living and to be the driving force behind the agricultural economy.

Though important, cultivation of the olive is not all this province has to offer. Jaén's fertile lowlands are among the best suited for the cultivation of Mediterranean cereals, while its mines have converted the towns of Linares and Andújar into two powerful industrial centres. Most impressive of all, however, are its

sierras of Cazorla and Segura, both of which are veritable ecological havens whose fossilised green landscapes covered the entire peninsula in Roman times. Fire has been no match for the constant regeneration of these sierras' flora; and less still the axe which chopped away for centuries in order to provide wood for building ships. All species of Mediterranean fauna, and flora endemic to the region thrive here untouched by pollution. Protected areas, they play a vital role in preserving animal species in danger of extinction.

The key to Jaén's history and evolution as a city is obvious at a glance. From its rocky perch, the imposing castle of Santa Catalina is a clear indication of the city's strategic importance at the crossroads that this region has always been. Called the `Holy Kingdom', Jaen was in the vanguard of the war between the Moors and the Christians, and then a gateway to Andalusia even during the Napoleonic campaigns. The founder of the Alhambra, al-Amar, who was from these parts, surrendered it to Ferdinand III as part of an astute vassalage pact, thereby allowing the Castilians to enter the two Andalusias.

Dating from this period of the 13th century is the reconstruction of the magnificent castle which now houses a parador, one of the state-owned chain of luxury hotels. Panoramic views of the city and surrounding countryside are commanded from its heights. Clearly distinguished is the solemn presence of the cathedral *(below and previous page)* with its elegant façade flanked by sturdy towers Converted from a mosque into a church in 1368, work did not begin on the cathedral until 1500. A delay due to lack of funds meant that the architect responsible for its construction, Andrés de Vandelvira, student of Siloé, was able to design it in the new Renaissance style (1536). Work continued for 20 years until Vandelvira's death, after which nothing was done for a further 80 years.

In spite of the gradual appearance of the Baroque, and especially in its interior, the cathedral retains its classical Renaissance flavour, a fact that is especially evident in the Sacristy where Vandelvira managed to create a veritable masterpiece of Spanish architecture.

Above, the castle of Iruela set in a landscape of olive groves
On the right, detail from the Jabalquinto Palace, below left, the fountain in the Plaza Santa María. Below, right the façade of the Council building.

Previous page (above), interior of the Cathedral, and below, the Cathedral.

Úbeda

After the battle of Las Navas de Tolosa (1212), the history of Andalusia was to undergo a radical change. The people of the Castilian tableland could not get over their surprise, or greed, as they surveyed the fertile and generous Andalusia below them. Úbeda and Baeza, already much disputed in the past, were converted into mainstays of the Christian "Advance" and, thus, into two Castilian towns. Indeed, such was the extent of their appropriation that even Romanesque art was to leave its mark on them. The advancing frontiers gave them the opportunity to establish themselves firmly in the rearguard position as a stronghold of the new era. The local aristocratic families, already the owners of great estates, battled to establish their power by building mediaeval palaces and by transforming old mosques into modern Gothic churches. However, and strange though it may seem, their finest hour was to be lived under the great patrons of the 16th century after the conquest of Granada. Úbeda was transformed into an artistic and cultural centre by the secretary of the Emperor Charles V, Francisco de Cobos, a figure who could well be considered Prime Minister of the Empire. The all-embracing power of the mediaeval nobility, clipped by the Catholic Monarchs, was

to be given a new lease of life in the lineages that offered their support to the Emperor. As such, the noble families merely emulated the Italian trend, governing the fate of the Empire in the same way as Italian families governed the republics. The parallel is very clear: the Plaza de Vázquez de Molina in Úbeda is neither a town square nor a Castilian public enclosure; rather, it is a family space. As such, it was not the town's church but a family funeral chapel that was built around it. In the same way as Charles V built his tomb in Granada (the Cathedral), Francisco de Cobos, whose income was even higher than that of the Emperor himself, had his own private tomb built in the Capilla Panteon de El Salvador. Similarly, just as Diego de Siloé was designing the Puerta del Perdón ("Penitent's Gate") in Granada, his student Valdelvira, taking his inspiration from the latter, set to work on the façade of El Salvador copying not only the structure, but the symbols themselves the triumphal arch, the allegories of Faith and Justice, the large family coats of arms, the mythology charged with symbolism, the transfiguration of Christ with which it was crowned etc. Inside the church, the tomb's layout a round chapel crowned by a dome was also copied from the Capilla Mayor. Valdelvira was an accomplished and highly trained architect who liked to be on site during construction. Here he was accompanied by the interior decorator, Jannette who had come from Fountainebleau where feminine decoration was becoming increasingly popular. This would explain why the sacristy gives the impression of a French ballroom with its hanging vaults and medallions, elements that were especially alien to Siloé and his contemporaries.

Next to El Salvador, indeed practically flanking it, is the palace of the Ortega family which is today a parador known as Condestable Dávalos. Here also Vandelvira managed to give its façade a touch of Renaissance sobriety almost antici-

pating the future style of Herrera. More austere still, however, is the façade of the neighbouring Palacio de las Cadenas ("the Chains") which was built for the secretary of Philip II. Today the Town Hall, its inner courtyard is among the finest courtyards of the Spanish Renaissance.

However, Úbeda was also to experience turbulent times. Razed to the ground by Mohammed V, it was to stage the battles between Peter I and his step-brother Henry, constable Dávalos and favourite of John II who was put to death in the end by the latter. It stood up to Cisneros and supported the comuneros (rebels who confronted Charles I). The church of Santa María de los Reales Alcázares, situated on the other side of the square, is a good exponent of its own history. A whole range of styles are combined here from Hispano-Muslim to Baroque, Gothic-Mudéjar and Renaissance.

This church is not the only example in Úbeda of mixed styles and pasts. The church of San Pablo was also a mosque and if some of its capitals are Romanesque, the south façade is a beautiful example of the Late Gothic, while its Plateresque tower is reminiscent of many other towers that watch over the Castilian tablelands.

The same could also be said for the church of San Pedro and indeed for the many other churches San Isidoro, San Lorenzo, Santo Domingo, Trinidad etc. that contribute to Úbeda's status as a combination of masterpieces of the Spanish Renaissance.

BAEZA

Although not as wealthy when it comes to monuments, Úbeda's small and neighbouring "twin sister" nevertheless possesses a stately charm that is more approachable, less imposing. This town is also perched high on a hill from which it dominates the extensive stretch of fields surrounding it, a fact that explains why it was one of the first towns to be re-conquered (1227). Baeza is full of surprises, starting with the Plaza de los Leones, so-called for the Roman fountain at its centre, the double Arco de Villalar, raised in honour of Charles V, the Casa del Pópulo and the Antigua Carnicería ("Old Butcher's"). The latter two buildings demonstrate Baeza's early vocation as a great city: a simple butcher's shop is adorned with the proud presence of an Imperial coat of arms, while its large windows look as if they belong to a noble residence than to a drying place for skins. Similarly, the Town Hall close to this square bears an outstanding Renaissance façade which seems out of place when we consider that this building was no more than a prison in its heyday. Moving into the town centre along narrow mediaeval streets, passing under archways and colonnades, we might be taken aback as we round a corner by the façade of the Palacio de Jabalquinto whose Gothic elegance rivals any other to be found in Guadalajara or Salamanca. Directly opposite is the church of Santa Cruz, the only Romanesque church in Andalusia, while the Cathedral (of Santa María), which was founded by Ferdinand III over the foundations of a mosque, is within a short walking distance. It also houses the bishop's palace. Vandelvira himself was responsible for the design, while two of its wrought-iron grilles were fashioned by the master forger, Bartolomé, from Jaén. The poet Antonio Machado gave classes in the neighbouring Universidad Antigua which dates from the 16th century. The town also contains numerous convents and churches, some of which are of the very first order, making Baeza one of the most interesting ensembles in Spain.

Previous page, above, Plaza de Sta. María. Below, wide-angle view of the vault in the Hospital de Santiago

On this page above, the façade of the church of el Salvador, below, details of the church

Sculptured coats of arms of the Cobos family on the classical façade which also contains allegorial sculptures

Jaén's 'silver' landscape is a veritable sea of olive trees; and yet we tend to forget, although fortunately less now than before, that it is home to four natural parks including the largest park in the country covering more than 300,000 hectares of protected terrain: Cazorla, Segura-Las Villas as well as Despeñaperros, Sierra de Andújar and Sierra Mágina. It also has two nature reserves, Laguna (lagoon) del Chinche and Laguna Honda, close to Alcaudete, not to mention various nature spots such as the Upper Guadalquivir. Top, view of Cazorla park surrounding the Castillo de la Yedra

which dominates the access to the Sierra and to its important timber resources, one of the reasons why this village was so important in the Christian reconquest.

Above these lines, the village of Baños de La Encina with the imposing Caliphal castle that, dating from the 9th century, was intended to defend the nearby Despeñaperros pass.

Below left, Segura de la Sierra, eagles' nest (and there are Imperial eagles in the area) overlooking the river Guadalquivir.

Below, view of Alcaudete, land of the queen of all olives the `picúa´, a species which is pointed at one end, and close to Martos, the world's leading producer of olive oil.

ALMERIA

Sheltered at the foot of the valley formed by the sierras of Gádor and Gata is the city of Almeria whose name in Arabic means "looking glass of the sea". A port before it was a city, civilisations as far back as the Bronze Age came here more than 4,500 years ago in search of metals such as the much coveted tin. 25 km north is Los Millares where the extremely important metalworking culture was born. Close by is El Algar whose famous bell-shaped glass would find its way over much of Central Europe. Almeria's strategic position made it the chief sea-port of the Cordovan Caliphate, a fact borne out in Abd al-Rahman III's commissioning of a shipyard for the Caliphate's boats, and of the Alcazaba in 995, the latter being one of the largest military fortresses to be built in the Middle Ages. A veritable umbilical cord between the Caliphate and the East, all Mediterranean trade passed through its port. Boats for the purpose were built here and Muslims squadrons organised, their progress leading to such maritime advances as the caravel, advances which ended up facilitating the Castilians' crossing of the Atlantic Ocean.

On the fall of the Caliphate, Almeria's powerful maritime position ensured its survival as the capital of a culturally splendid taifa kingdom until 1147 when the Christians conquered the city for the first time. These were aided by other maritime powers eager to control the commercial route to Genoa, the presence and influence of which being evident in the region throughout the Early Middle Ages. The Christians' definitive conquest took place in 1489 and with it Almeria's great decline, geopolitical interest having shifted to the Atlantic as a result of the American adventure. Berber pirates, aided by groups of banished Moriscos, continued to attack the city, a fact which explains why its Gothic-Renaissance cathedral, designed by Siloé, looks more like a fortress than a church; it even possesses underground wells that were intended to ensure survival in case of siege. Its decline was inevitable, however, and so much so that in 1658, after another earthquake had shaken the region, only 500 inhabitants remained in the city alive. It was only at the end of the 20th century that Almeria began to show signs of recovery with the 'intervention' of the so-called "Almerian miracle" of intensive greenhouse farming.

The most impressive monument in Almeria is the Alcazaba or castle, whose walls follow the hills and hollows around it to a length of over half a kilometre and effectively divide it into three parts. Between the outer and middle walls was a buffer zone which might have been used as a refuge for the townspeople in times of siege and which was controlled and watched over from above. Now it is filled with attractive gardens. The second or middle part contains remains of both military and civilian buildings. At the heart of the Alcazaba was the mosque which would have been converted into a church after the conquest of the city. The entire Alcazaba comprises a magnificent platform overlooking and dominating the whole city.

Fortunately, in recent times Almeria has progressed from being one of the most economically depressed parts of Spain to become the market garden of Europe in the 21st century, with its out-of-season fruit and vegetables grown under a `sea of plastic', taking full advantage of the more than 3,000 hours of sunshine it enjoys every year.

Above, entrance to the Alcazaba. Below, country cottage near Garrucha that is typical of popular architecture in Almería.

This brilliant landscape is a modern addition to the older exotic and varied countryside, unique for the contrasts it provides and which made the region of Almeria the centre for filming Westerns during the 1960s. From the city, one might draw an imaginary line towards the East, to the Cabo de Gata-Nijar natural park, the only desert within Europe, where palm trees grow and where the mountains descend to the transparent, coral-reefed waters of the Mediterranean, and where their inaccessibility for motorized transport makes the beaches places of peace and tranquility. To the West is the agricultural area where a green miracle has been worked.

Above left, the village of Ohanes in the Almerían Alpujarras tucked away between mountains and irrigated lands. On the right, Tabernas from whose castle the snow-white peaks of the Sierra Nevada can be discerned, as well as the spectacular desert that lies at its foot. Below right, Mini-Hollywood setting for countless Westerns. Below, foot, Mojácar.

Above these lines, border of the cereal growing lands at Gerjal on the edge of the desert. Below, the castle at Vélez Blanco. The courtyard was removed stone by stone to become one of the most valued exhibits in New York's Metropolitan Museum.

Above, Cabo de Gata and its cliffs. This cape is at the heart of the Cabo de Gata-Nijar Park which covers an area of 29,000 hectares and encompasses the neighbouring east coast formed by dunes, isolated beaches and coves. To the west stretch the salinas or salt water lagoons (left), an area rich in semi-desert flora and a haven for aquatic birds. Right, Almería's desert.

CÁDIZ

From the Tartessian culture, taking in such marvels in time as a Phoenician capital or the much-celebrated anthropomorphic sarcophagi, to its protagonism in more recent times, Cádiz has accumulated more than 3,000 years of history under its mariner's belt. A Phoenician capital and Carthaginian trading station, it was conquered by the Romans, Muslims and Christians (Alfonso X in 1262). As a keel moving out to sea, it opened its gates to the New World and provided a bridge to Africa. Attacked by the English from the time of Philip II to Trafalgar (1804), it laughed in the face of the French soon after, and, without losing its smile, became the seat of the Spanish liberal government, the Cortes, in 1812 serving as a model for the rest of Europe.

With a coastline over 250 km long, and a surface area covering over 7,000 km, Cádiz's seafaring province is surprisingly varied. It has a share in the Sistema Subbético with a mountainous region in the north-east dotted with white towns and villages whose castles are reached via the most enchanting of winding streets adorned with freshly whitewashed balconies and courtyards: ARCOS DE LA FRONTERA, UBRIQUE, SETENIL, ALGODONALES, ZAHARA, OLVERA, etc. Paradises for inland rural tourism yet removed from standard tourist routes, their traditional charm remains almost entirely intact. At the tip of the province lies GRAZALEMA, known for its Spanish firs, its hunting and its lush green landscapes, themselves the result of the heavy rainfal here a welcome gift that characterises the area (more than 2,000 c.c. a year). We are further enchanted by our visit to the seigniorial town of MEDINA SIDONIA, to JIMENA DE LA FRONTERA, to the ghost town of CASTELLAR DE LA FRONTERA, and to the little whitewashed village of VEJER that, perched on a rock high above us, looks more like a nest full of doves. From the border towns of the old Nasrid kingdom, the route of the toro bravo (fighting bull) moves into the countryside surrounding Gibraltar passing through TARIFA

and over the Laguna de la Janda where a whole kingdom was lost in 711, an event that was to have such an important impact on the history of Spain. The SIERRA CARBONERA, watched over by new giants of the "wind mill" variety whose function is to produce energy, LOS BARRIOS, the port of ALGECIRAS on the threshold of Africa, and the proud SAN ROQUE that never loses sight of the Rock silhouetted against the horizon.

Cádiz is bordered by LOS PUERTOS, SAN FERNANDO, the shipyards, the salt pans, the Bay and, above all, the PUERTO DE SANTO MARÍA and JEREZ. The latter is home to Spain's best-known and most international wines. From here to SANLÚCAR our spirits are lifted by the penetrating aroma of wine that perfumes the air. Bacchus would have no desire for any other Olympus. Jerez's chalky soil and Atlantic winds combine to produce the best manzanilla (dry sherry) in the world. The production of sherry is a legend in itself and one that is not without a certain degree of mystery. The early grape harvest takes place in September; the grapes are left out in the sun and then pressed. The temperature of the resulting juice or mosto ("must") is rigorously controlled as it ferments; it is then shaken, cleaned and deposited in American oak casks. The chemical composition may be identical in two neighbouring casks, but only the sensitive sense of smell of the taster will discover and determine the variety of sherry to which each belongs. This could be a light, dry fino that is pale in colour, or a more mature amontillado, or indeed an excellent-quality palo cortado. Or it could be a completely different oloroso or an unbeatable, sweet Pedro Ximénes. An entire production chain, where not a single link can fail, is accompanied by the patient labour of time for the miracle to be complete. As far as white wines are concerned, the sherry variety is the only one that matures in barrels.

Jerez has an important architectural heritage as is to be expected of a city with such an aristocratic background: the 18th-century collegiate church of

Above, aerial view of Cádiz surrounded by water, the "little silver cup" as it is familiarly referred to. On the left, Puerta Tierra, the old entrance gate leading into the walled city of Cádiz.

San Salvador *(above)* displays a combination of Mudéjar influences, the churches of San Miguel and Santiago, built in typically Andalusian flamboyant Gothic style, the castle which preserves some sections of the city's enclosure wall from thc 12th century etc. As well as being the horse capital of Spain, Jerez has been the point of reference and seat of Flamenco from the time of the latter's uncertain origins at the beginning of the 19th century when it emerged in the city's gypsy quarters, to the creation, in the 20th century, of a professorship dedicated to the art. Signs of Jerez's modernity are evidenced in its racing circuit and in the rock music festival known as Asparagus Rock held annually in the city.

Above left, collegiate church of El Salvador in Jerez (granted the status of Cathedral in 1980) with its beautiful piers and flying buttresses. The grape harvest feast is celebrated here every September. Above these lines, the clock tower of the church of Santa María in Arcos de la Frontera. Of Visigothic origin, this church dominates the Plaza del Castillo. Below, Cádiz's beach at low tide. Below left, one of the old sherry "cathedrals".

This page shows different aspects of the province of Cádiz's varied geography. Above, the castle of Medina Sidonia which dominates, from its hilltop perch, the pastureland valley that stretches out to the sea (in the background). Above these lines, the Sierra Carbonera dotted with modern windmills transforming the strong winds from the Strait into electric energy. On the left, Plaza de Tarifa which has an african air about it, and on the right, ruins of the Roman town of Bolonia (now Bella) next to the beach where 2,000 years ago tuna was already being salted. Below, the small bay of the Costa de Conil sheltering pleasure boats from the wind.

Situated on the outskirts of the city, Jerez's Cartuja de la Defensión resumed its activity as a monastery over fifty years ago. This Charterhouse was founded in 1463 when the Carthusian order had gained an importance that was unrivalled in the rest of Spain. It has a magnificent Gothic cloister of 1478. The monastery reached its zenith in the 16th and 17th centuries when the Baroque façade was built, its exquisite decoration contrasting greatly with the austerity of the monks' cells. Also built during this period was the Claustro de los Muertos (great cloister) which is surrounded by pines, and the Claustrillo (small cloister) around the church. In 1835, and as with all ecclesiastical wealth across the country, this monastery's treasures were confiscated, a fate to which it had already been subjected 25 years previously at the time of the secularisation of church wealth enforced by the Napoleonic troops during the War of Independence. One can still imagine the sad departure of the monastery's last monk accompanied by two silver-white, strong and agile horses, the last remaining specimens of Spanish thoroughbreds that the Carthusian monks had been breeding since the 14th century. It was for this monastery that Francisco de Zurbarán painted his famous Carthusian monk paintings which today hang in the museums of Cádiz and Seville.

Since the beginning of the 21st century, women are also permitted to visit this monument following a decision on the part of the Church authorities to lift previous restrictions.

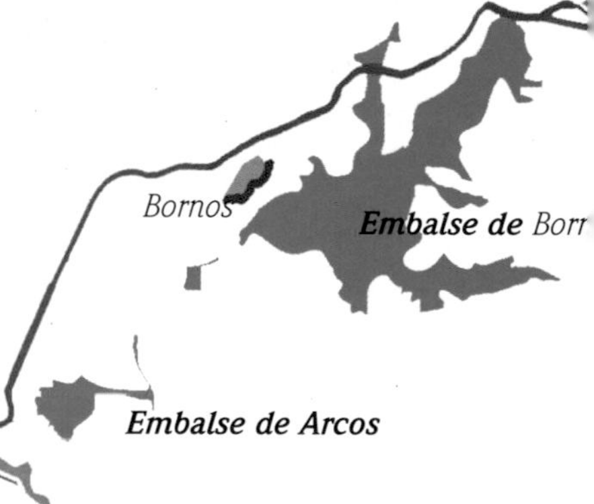

The Route of the White Villages, *which features more than a dozen of them, extends into the province of Málaga to include Ronda. The villages on this route are known for having once formed the old border of Granada's Nasrid kingdom. Clinging to the slopes of mountain peaks, the brilliant white of their buildings stands out against a background of green forests that are planted with cork-oaks, chestnuts and holm-oaks. Above,* Castellar, *fighting bull*

Above, spring-time view of Jimena de la Frontera. On the right, Zahara with the Sierra de Grazalema in the background. Immediatly below, another view of Arcos from the lookout of its square, and at the foot of the page, Grazalema, home to the Spanish fir and known for its high rainfall. Between, Vejer de la Frontera which overlooks the Atlantic.

The town of NIEBLA is known more for its sailors who accompanied Columbus and less for its church of Santa María de la Granada, a former mosque from which it retains many elements including the mihrab. On the left, the ablutions courtyard, and on the right, the Mudéjar tower which was the former minaret. Even more surprising is the survival of the 10th-century Caliphal mosque in ALMO-NASTER LA REAL in the province of Huelva (centre left) with its original capitals (next to these lines) similar to those found in the Great Mosque of Cordova . Below, the beaches of PUNTA UMBRÍA next to an important industrial site constructed in the environs of Huelva, birthplace of the Turdetan and Tartessian cultures. For centuries Huelva has been a seafaring region that few would rival, Columbus himself recruiting his crew from the sailors here.

HUELVA

Above these lines, the 36-metre high monument of Columbus looking out into infinity that was erected in 1929 at the mouth of the Tinto River. Below, Mudéjar cloister in the monastery of La Rábida.

The Sierra Morena mountain range serves as a hinge between the Meseta (table-land covering most of the regions of Castile and Leon, Castile-La Mancha and Extremadura) and Andalusia. Beyond this spinal column, Andalusia extends its roots from Lower Spain in the north right down to the sea in the south. Situated in the west of Andalusia is the province of Huelva whose mountainous northern portion meets Extremadura in the Sierra de Aracena y Picos de Aroche, a Natural Park since 1989 covering an area of over 180,000 hectares that is dotted with white towns and villages nestling in forests planted with chestnuts, oaks and holm-oaks. This is the land of the cerdo ibérico (Iberian pig), its climatic conditions and particular flora and micro-fauna ensuring a natural production of the best cured ham in the world. Apart from Jabugo, the white villages dedicated to the production of this culinary marvel are Alájar, a magnificent example of popular architecture surrounded by cork-oaks, AROCHE, which is still enclosed within fortification walls, ALMONASTER, known for its mosque, CORTEGANA, CUMBRES MAYORES, ARACENA and its cave. The most industrial city in Andalusia, Huelva is situated at the confluence of the rivers Tinto and Odiel where thousands of years ago civilisation entered the peninsula in search of copper deposits. These mines had probably a lot to do with the emergence of the Tartessian culture, while the mythical Atlantis could not have been far from the marshes. However, Huelva's history is inextricably linked to the discovery of America, the crew, caravels and experience with which Columbus set sail originating from such seafaring towns as Palos de Moguer, birthplace of the writer Juan Ramón Jiménez, and Niebla which still conserves some of its 46 medieval towers and was the first place where gunpowder was used in 1224. However, the most important Columbus-related centre is the monastery of La Rábida without whose support, and especially that of Brother Juan Pérez de Marchena who managed to convince Queen Isabella, Columbus would never have been able to set sail.

Alajar

Aracena

Huelvan holm-oaks

As with many other Christianised feasts, the celebration of the Rocío pilgrimage has its origin in pagan antiquity, set as it is against a background of spring celebrations that affirm agricultural activity in the surrounding marshlands. It began with the construction of the hermitage that Alfonso X (the Wise) dedicated to Santa María de las Rocinas in the 13th century. The miraculous apparition of the Virgin in the 15th century served to breathe new life into the Marian tradition, the latter firmly rooting itself in popular worship from the 17th century. Today it has become a phenomenon of the masses, and one that is difficult for the outsider to comprehend.About a million people gather together on Whit Monday to celebrate the feast of El Rocío in a pilgrimage that lasts

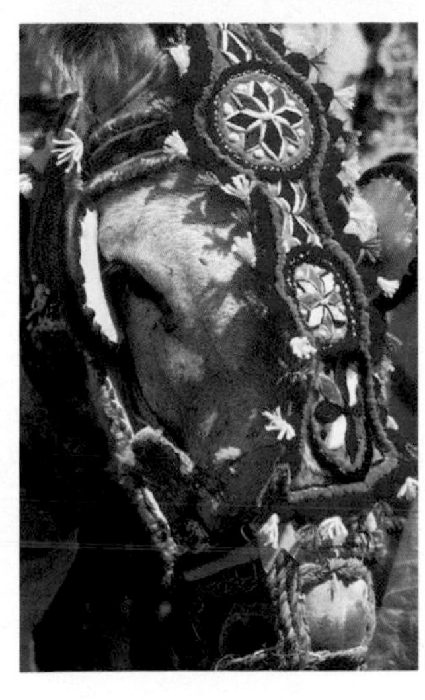

lasts various days and whose religious significance, for the majority of pilgrims, goes beyond the desire and need to be reunited with Nature. Above, mass celebrated on Whit Sunday. On the left page, the Simpecado (banner bearing the Virgin's image) which, marking the Camino (way), the pilgrims follow on foot, and the ferry crossing of the river at Sanlúcar de Barrameda. On this page, the marshland setting and festivities that accompany the pilgrimage.

Contents

Direción y realización: J. Agustín Núñez Guarde
Supervisión editorial: Miguel Román Vega
Revisión editorial: Giulia Fernández Avagliano
Edición, diseño y maquetación: Edilux ®
Fotografía: Edilux, (J. Agustín Núñez y Miguel Román)
Redacción: Edilux ©
Textos de la Alhambra: Aurelio Cid ©
Textos del Palacio de Carlos V : Concepción Felez Lubelza ©
Fotomecánica y fococomposición: Edilux
Ilustraciones de Granada: Miguel Salvatierra ©
Infografía de la Mezquita de Córdoba: Pablo Román
Planos de Andalucía: (2-3) Córdoba (78-79) y Sevilla (50-51): Vidal y Vidal
Fotografía aérea de la Alhambra: Daniel Draco
Fotografía página 5 abajo: Laurent. Archivo Ruiz Vernacci IPHE
Fotografía aérea de Cádiz: Oronoz
Impresión: Copartgraf
Encuadernación: Hermanos Olmedo

ISBN: 8487282-60-1
D.L: GR-704/2000

Distribución: Edilux. Telf y fax: 0034-958-184056
E-mail: edilux@ctv.es